The

THINK LIGHT!
Lowfat Living Plan

Greg Phillips, M.S.

Speaking of Fitness, Inc.
Durango, Colorado

Caution: *Before starting any physical fitness and/or weight control program you should consult with your doctor.*

FOURTH EDITION

Published by Speaking of Fitness, Inc., 98 Everett Dr., Suite C, Durango, Colorado 81301.

Printed in the USA on recycled paper
February 1991

FOREWORD

As a cardiologist, I believe that many of the people I see in my office probably wouldn't be needing my help if they had learned the principles of lowfat living at an early age. I also believe that it's never too late to improve one's lifestyle habits.

That's why I highly recommend The THINK LIGHT! - Lowfat Living Plan. THINK LIGHT! is a sensible, easy-to-follow strategy for developing healthier lifestyle routines and patterns. The THINK LIGHT! - Lowfat Living Plan teaches us to take responsibility for our health. There are no quick fixes or magic pills in this program. THINK LIGHT! is a simple, common sense approach to daily living that reminds us of the importance of a wholesome diet, regular aerobic exercise, and a positive state of mind. Read it, enjoy it, and by all means, do it!

Steven P. Van Camp, MD, FACSM
Alvarado Medical Group
San Diego, CA

To Jan, Chelsea & Bryce

Contents

INTRODUCTION

Y OU'RE overfat, and you're frustrated about it. It's a situation that you find difficult to deal with. It's fair to say you probably would be happier with yourself if weight wasn't an issue in your life. You've tried to correct the problem more than once before. You've gone on diets, joined weight control programs, taken exercise classes, maybe even sought counseling. More than likely you've had your share of success. Unfortunately, it was only temporary. So here you are, once again, caught up in the same old, tiring struggle to get your weight under control.

One thing's for certain; you're not alone. It doesn't take a Gallup poll to tell you that the majority of Americans are overfat. All you have to do is look around the next time you're at the shopping center. It's obvious. We're in pretty bad shape. Over a third of the people in this country are obese; while another thirty-three percent are seriously struggling to keep their weight from getting out of control.

FOCUS ON FITNESS

The irony is that our culture has never before been so fixated on physical fitness. It's everywhere. We read about fitness in the newspapers, hear about it on radio talk shows, and see it covered on the evening network news. The grocery store racks are filled with fitness magazines, all adorned with beautiful bodies and headlines promising to make you leaner, meaner, faster, and fitter. When it comes to fashion, the fit look is in. The latest clothing styles are designed to show it off. Diet books and exercise videos continue to make the bestseller lists. And it doesn't stop there. These days fitness is used to sell everything from cigarettes to chicken soup to panty hose.

Whether we like it or not, physical fitness has made it big in America. And it's here to stay. It's a wonderful, positive phenomenon for those who have chosen to get involved. It's an added source of frustration for those who haven't. There's nothing worse than feeling dissatisfied with yourself and being reminded about it everywhere you look. With so much focus on fitness, it's not as acceptable as it once was to be overfat. Call it an increased health awareness. Call it peer pressure. Call it vanity. Whatever you call it, there are a lot of frustrated overfat people in this country.

An obvious question is why do people continue to stay overfat if it makes them so frustrated? Three possible answers are (1) they don't truly desire to change, (2) they simply don't know

how to begin to get rid of excess fat, or (3) they
don't believe they can lose fat since they've tried
before with limited success. Most likely, the real
answer involves all three.

IT'S HABITS THAT COUNT

Granted, for someone who's been overfat all
her life it's no easy task to solve the problem once
and for all. Most people don't suddenly become
overfat. It's a medical fact that the majority of
weight problems are the result of faulty habits,
not faulty glands. Years of unhealthy eating habits and a lack of consistent exercise are responsible for the accumulation of excess body fat.

If you're not satisfied with the shape you're
in, your habits are probably to blame. Next to
genes, lifestyle habits are the most powerful
shapers of the human body. Eating habits. Shopping habits. Cooking habits. Exercise habits.
Even thinking habits. Day in and day out, it's
these repetitive patterns and routines in our lives
that determine whether we're tight and toned or
soft and flabby.

The truth is, we look like we live. That's why
the only way to permanently get rid of excess fat is
to permanently get rid of the habits that caused
fat to be there in the first place. Temporary dieting is a waste of time and energy. Diets don't
change habits. The overwhelming majority of
people regain their excess body fat once they re-

turn to their previous eating habits.

The habits that are required to develop a lean, physically fit body are well understood. There's no secret to it. Lean people live lowfat lives. Their lifestyle habits condition their bodies not to accumulate excessive amounts of body fat. In a nutshell, lean people eat right and exercise regularly. And **they're consistent about it**. By developing the kind of lifelong eating and exercise habits that work for them, instead of against them, they're able to permanently make weight control a "non-issue" in their lives.

A FEW WORDS ABOUT CHANGE

In theory it all sounds pretty simple. Change your habits, and you'll change your body. Of course, we all know how hard it is to change old habits, particularly when it comes to the way we eat. Yet, it is possible and people do succeed. We've all heard success stories from friends, family, or acquaintances. In all cases, something clicks and the person decides it's time to make a change in their life. With determination, they gradually make the changes necessary to live the life of a lean person. In time, their body follows suit.

Unfortunately, the success stories seem to be far and few between. The reason has to do with our attitudes about change. In general, people have a hard time changing. It's easier not to. We say things like, "I'm just not ready to change yet" or "Now's not a good time for me to try to change." A decision to change is a decision to take a risk. Change requires a step from the familiar to the unfamiliar; from the known to the unknown. It requires confidence, commitment, sacrifice, determination, and self-discipline. Pretty scary stuff! As surprising as it may sound, overfat people often think the process of change will make them even more miserable than their weight problem does. Who wants to trade a little misery for a lot of misery?

The good news is that change doesn't have to be such a horrible creature. The horror is really only in our minds. It's an illusion we create to give us reason to stay right where we are, to protect ourselves from having to confront something we prefer not to deal with. We prefer stability over instability, order over disorder, comfort over discomfort. So we place our notion of change in psychologically constructed haunted houses, battlefields, and toxic waste sites. We don't know exactly what will happen if we try to change, but we're afraid it may be unpleasant. All the more reason to stay away.

Change isn't frightening or scary. It's not good nor bad, hard nor easy. Change is not a feeling or an emotion. Change is simply a process. It's a natural part of living. It happens. How we **react** to it is a personal decision. We make the choice of which emotional label we stick on it. We decide whether to embrace change or to do battle with it.

LEARNING LOWFAT HABITS

For most, living a lowfat life means making some important lifestyle changes; changes in the way you think, changes in how you eat, and changes in how you exercise. It may sound overwhelming, but rest assured; it isn't. In the last decade millions of Americans have successfully made the change to lowfat living. You can too, if you're willing to try.

Making the change to lowfat living is a process for you to experience and enjoy. The easiest way to go about it is to take one step at a time. If you try to hurry change, the chances are you'll never get there. Change moves at its own pace. Once you understand and accept this fact, you can help, rather than hinder, the process. It helps to remember that once you've learned the right habits, they are yours forever.

THE SIX KEYS TO CHANGE

Imagine the process of change as a journey down a winding path. At the end of this path stands an enormous door through which you must pass. When you get to the other side you will forever experience the joy of a lean, physically fit body. No more excess body fat. No more struggles with willpower. Beyond this door lie the pleasures of lowfat living.

The only problem is that the door is bolted with six padlocks. To get through the door, you must unlock it with the **"six keys to change."** Fortunately for you, all six keys can be found along the winding path leading to the door. Your goal is to travel along the path and find the six keys to change.

THE SIX KEYS TO CHANGE:

- True Desire
- Strong Belief
- Knowledge
- A Plan for Change
- Setbacks
- Progress

How will you know where to look? Don't worry, the six keys to change are easy to recognize and easy to find. The trick is to hang on to them once you have them in your grasp. The keys to change can be slippery. You may end up finding one of the keys, losing it for awhile, and then finding it all over again. It's all part of the process of change. When all six keys are firmly in hand you'll have no problem passing through the door of change.

TRUE DESIRE

Do you have the desire to improve your eating habits? Do you desire a leaner, healthier body? Does changing your lifestyle to include more exercise sound desirable to you? Hopefully you can answer yes to all three questions because the process of change begins the moment you consciously acknowledge your **desire** to change. The stronger your desire, the greater the likelihood of success.

True desire, the kind of desire that is necessary to make change happen, is wanting something so much that you're willing to confront your fears to get it. Fear of failure. Fear of sacrifice. Fear of commitment. Alone or together, fears are bullies that try to stop us from succeeding. Without desire to bolster our courage, it's easy to be intimidated by fears and head back to the security of familiar territory.

STRONG BELIEF

People who have been fighting the weight control battle for a number of years are often a bit "gun shy" when it comes to starting a new fat-loss program. The desire to lose fat may be strong, but the negative reinforcement of previously unsuccessful attempts may be even stronger. Nothing is more disheartening than facing the self-imposed guilt and disappointment that comes from an unsuccessful attempt to lose fat. Especially when the attempt began in earnest with all sorts of sincere self-promises.

Studies show that a person's attitude going into a weight control program is a major factor in determining whether the outcome is success or failure. For this reason, it is important that along with desire, you **strongly believe** you will succeed at change. Beliefs are merely mental pictures you've created and chosen to accept. If you believe you will fail, then you will. Richard Bach, in his book *Illusions*, said, "Argue for your limitations, and sure enough they'll be yours..." The reverse is also true. If you believe success is possible, then success is already yours. As Bach says, "You're not given a wish without the power to make it come true..."

KNOWLEDGE

If belief and desire propel you forward, it's **knowledge** that guides you on the path of change, particularly if the path leads to lowfat living. Before you can turn your weight control dreams into reality, you must have a basic understanding of diet, of exercise, and, most importantly, of yourself. An understanding of *proven* and *legitimate* weight control principles is necessary to keep you headed in the right direction. Belief and desire are powerless when you're being reeled in by the myriad of fad diet books and quick fat-loss schemes that repeatedly show up on the market. The majority of these programs are designed to appeal to us on an emotional level, hitting us with the "something-for-nothing" approach. The quick and easy way out is always hard to resist.

Also hard to resist is the irrational notion that change is possible simply at the flick of a switch. We think to ourselves, "That's it. From this day on I'm only eating fresh fruits and vegetables until I get down to my ideal weight." Of course, it rarely works that way. Eating habits are usually the result of years and years of patterns and routines. Like a cave carved from the relentless pounding of the ocean, our minds and bodies become ingrained with developed tastes, preferences, and eating behaviors. It's unrealistic to expect to suddenly and immediately change that which has taken a lifetime to establish. Armed with a basic understanding of proven weight control principles and a general knowledge of the process of change, you can make practical and realistic lifestyle choices.

A PLAN FOR CHANGE

Once you have desire, belief, and knowledge tucked under your belt, you're ready to develop and implement **a plan for change**. A plan for change is a strategy for achieving results. It's the specific methods and techniques that you will use to change your habits. For example, your plan for change might include joining a health club and working out four days a week in the afternoons.

A good plan breaks the process of change

into a number of small steps. Instead of starting off with four workouts a week, you might try beginning with two or three days. After a few weeks you can add another daily workout to your schedule. Taking one step at a time, as opposed to the "all-or-nothing" approach, makes it possible to set realistic and attainable goals. This approach also gives you a basis for recognizing and rewarding your progress along the way.

A plan for change provides a "home base" to come back to in the event you get sidetracked along the way. It also includes specific contingency plans for overcoming the types of problems you're most likely to encounter. If you tend to be short on motivation when it comes to exercise, your plan could include getting a friend to join the health club with you. In short, having a carefully thought out plan for change creates a blueprint to follow that makes it easy for you to succeed.

SETBACKS

Once you've embarked upon your plan for change, the only things standing between you and your goals are the **setbacks of change**. The most important lesson for you to learn is: *setbacks are necessary ingredients in the recipe of change.* There's no way around it. You're going to face them. You're going to mess up, experience roadblocks, temporarily fall short. You're going to have moments when you feel like giving up. You should anticipate them. The more ingrained the habit you're trying to change, the more setbacks you're likely to have. But don't take it personally. It's human nature. Ultimately, your success at change hinges upon your ability to become stronger from your setbacks, rather than weaker. Every time you experience a setback, consider it a lesson; and every lesson is an opportunity to advance closer to your goal. You have to fail to succeed. Change rarely makes an appearance when everything is going right. On the contrary, change awakens in the aftershock of disruption. Setbacks are an impetus to change.

When you try to change habits, the most self-destructive thing you can do when you have a setback is label yourself a failure. Negative self-judgement is simply an excuse for not trying anymore. It's a rationalization for giving up. "I failed, so I might as well quit now. I'll only fail again if I keep trying."

It's more productive to keep your emotions at bay when you catch yourself struggling to stay on track. Your struggle has no relation to your worthiness as a human being. Nor does it have anything to do with your ability to change. *How you respond* when you experience a setback is the issue, not the fact that it happened.

• The way to benefit when you get off track is to think of it as a mistake you've been given the chance to correct. Change comes when you've had practice correcting your mistakes. That's how you learn, isn't it; by correcting your mistakes? Trial and error? The more mistakes you make, the more practice you get at correcting them. Remember, there's no hurrying change. Everyone learns at their own pace. With enough practice you eventually learn to catch your mistakes before, not after, they happen. When you reach this point you've learned your lesson and the change is yours to keep.

PROGRESS

Besides using failure as an excuse to quit, people often sabotage their attempt to change by not acknowledging their **progress** along the way. We tend to measure progress in terms of whether or not we reach our final goal. Unfortunately, if our final goal is a long way off, we must wait a long time until we feel successful. Without positive reinforcement along the way, it's easy to give up, no matter how good our intentions.

It's important to reward the process of change, as much as the end result. The trip goes by much quicker and is more pleasurable if you enjoy the scenery as you go. Every step forward is a success since it takes you that much closer to your final goal. Learn to pat yourself on the back every time you catch yourself doing what you want to be doing. By acknowledging your progress along the way, you send a positive message to yourself. You deserve all the strokes you can give yourself. Feeling good about your accomplishments is the best way to keep you going forward.

Remember ...

Habits are powerful shapers of the human form. If you want to change your body, you need to change your habits.

Lean people live lowfat lives.

Change is a process. It is a journey in which important lessons are learned along the way. The easiest way to make the journey is by taking one step at a time.

There are six keys to change; True Desire, Strong Belief, Knowledge, A Plan for Change, Setbacks, Progress. When you're able to hold on to all six keys, change will be yours.

"The path to change has only two rules - Begin, and then Continue..."

Anonymous

The THINK LIGHT! Lowfat Living Plan

I_F you're thinking about heading down the path to changing your eating and exercise habits, you're probably wondering exactly where to begin. This is where Think Light! can help. Think Light! is a simple lowfat living plan. The Think Light! plan is based on the habits of millions of people who have learned to live lowfat lives. They're habits that will work for you, too. By incorporating the Think Light! habits into your lifestyle, you'll "re-program" your body to get rid of excess body fat.

There are only seven Think Light! habits for you to focus on. All seven habits share one thing in common; an emphasis on self-awareness. Whether it's buying food at the grocery store or going out for breakfast, living a lowfat life requires you to be aware of the choices you make. The

Think Light! habits help you make the right choices.
    The seven Think Light! habits fall into three
categories: Thinking Habits, Eating Habits, and
Exercise Habits.   The habits are all simple, but
don't let the simplicity fool you. You will feel and
see a remarkable difference in yourself when you
practice these Think Light! habits:

THE THINK LIGHT! HABITS

(1)   **Think Light! every day.**

(2)   **Keep the process of change moving forward
by recognizing and stopping negative self-
talk before it stops you.**

(3)   **Always remember; there's no such thing as
cheating.   There's   only   wandering.
Wandering is no excuse for quitting or self-
punishment.   It's   not   wrong   or   bad.
Wandering is normal.**

(4)   **If you want less fat on you, put less fat in
you.**

(5)   **Eat foods high in carbohydrate and fiber
with every meal or snack.**

(6)   **Eat less more often.**

(7)   **Make aerobic exercise a habit you enjoy.**

In the next seven chapters you'll learn more about each of the Think Light! habits. You'll find out that living the Think Light! lowfat life isn't complicated, nor does it require excessive planning, preparation, or willpower. It's no more difficult than living a high-fat life. All it takes is a conscious choice on your part.

Take the time to read each chapter slowly and carefully. The better you understand each habit, the easier it will be for you to incorporate them into your life. Remember, changing lifestyle habits is a process. The best approach is to take one step at a time.

If the going gets rough, think about the six keys to change. You must have all six to reach your destination. If you **truly desire** to make the Think Light! habits yours and you **strongly believe** it's possible, you're already on your way. In the chapters to come you'll gain the necessary **knowledge** of proper diet and exercise techniques. Your **plan for change** is to learn the seven Think Light! habits. All that's left for you to do is to keep moving forward. Remember, you're going to experience the **setbacks of change**; they're unavoidable. When you encounter them, learn from them, and move on. Most importantly, acknowledge your **progress** along the way. The journey is meant to be enjoyed.

Think Light! every day.

MENTAL VISUALIZATION

"Create a mental picture of how you most want to see yourself. Once you have, make sure you take a good look at your picture at least once a day. Keep in mind, if you can see where you're going, you'll probably get there."

FOR reasons not completely understood, mentally visualizing yourself succeeding helps move the process of change along more quickly. Perhaps it has to do with the fact that, outwardly, so much of our behavior is a product of what's going on in our subconscious minds. Learning to selectively place your thoughts and images into your subconscious mind enables you to more easily transform your ideas into reality.

Psychologists have theorized for years about how and why the subconscious mind exerts such a strong influence on conscious behavior. They do agree, however, that changing deeply ingrained habits and behaviors requires complete cooperation from all levels of the mind. Even with plenty of good intentions to back it up, the conscious mind is still not much of a match for an unruly subconscious.   When occupied with such undesirable tenants as fear, guilt, uncertainty, or anger the subconscious can be unmercifully manipulative and self-destructive.

Mental visualization offers you the opportunity to send in the "good guys" to bring peace and order to your subconscious. It's a healthy way to replace negative thought patterns with more positive ones.   For many, visualization provides a helpful boost of motivation and willpower. It can make the difference between quitting or hanging in there when the inevitable setbacks show up during the process of change.

Most people find it difficult to focus attention on a mental picture when their minds are running at their usual breakneck pace. A quiet mind is much more receptive to input than an active mind. For this reason, one of the best moments of the day for visualization is in the morning just as you're waking up while you're still in bed.   The idea is to take advantage of that peculiar state of semi-consciousness that lies somewhere between waking and sleeping, when you're aware that you're not completely asleep, yet not quite awake. This lazy, dreamlike state is a perfect time to Think Light! and sneak through the wide open doors of your subconscious mind a picture of the lean, firm, capable, happy, and confident person you want to be.

WHAT TO DO

(1) For you to achieve success through mental visualization you must first believe you will benefit from the experience. Decide that you are going to give the idea an honest try. The more open-minded you are, the better.

(2) Think about how you'd like to see yourself. Everyone's ideal self-image is different. Perhaps you picture yourself running down a country road: lean, strong, and physically fit. Maybe you see yourself looking great in a new outfit. Your image may show you preparing and enjoying a healthy meal. Whatever you choose, it is important that you create an image you feel completely comfortable with.

(3) Once you've established your mental picture, you're on your way. Before you go to sleep at night, take a moment to tell yourself that the first thought in your mind the next morning will be this picture. You may even want to stick a "Think Light!" note on your alarm clock. At first, you'll find that planting this evening reminder is necessary. However, once you get in the habit of starting your day with your visualization, you'll no longer need a nightly reminder .

(4) In the morning, at the moment you first realize you're waking up, turn your thoughts to the

image you've created. Completely immerse yourself in your picture. Visualize your picture in as much detail as possible, seeing each part of your body - your face, waist, hips, thighs, etc - as lean, strong, and fit. How does this new body make you feel? Imagine the sensation of being lighter than air... alive... warm... happy. If you see yourself moving, feel the breeze. Try to make the experience as real and as positive as you can. Most importantly, let yourself go, Think Light!, and enjoy the moment.

(5) If you have difficulty keeping your picture in focus at first, don't worry about it. Other thoughts or images will likely drift into your mind. When they do, just let them drift by and return to visualizing your picture. Some mornings, your image will be more difficult to conjure up. The busier you are, the harder it is to relax and enjoy the experience. On these days, take some deep breaths and relax your entire body from head to toe. As strange as it sounds, sometimes it helps to focus yourself by looking at the backs of your eyelids with your eyes closed. Or you might imagine a solid black chalk board. Every time a picture other than your desired image appears on the board, wipe it off.

(6) It doesn't matter how much time you spend visualizing. Each day will be different. What's

important is that you firmly implant this positive image in your mind, and feel good about it. With consistent practice and a commitment to the process of change, your image will soon become a reality.

Remember...

You'll have more success making changes in your life if you can create a clear image in your mind of exactly what you want to accomplish.

A quiet mind is more receptive than an active mind. One of the best moments of the day for visualization is in the morning just as you're waking up while you're still in bed.

Think Light! as often as you can.

Keep the process of change moving forward by recognizing and stopping negative self-talk before it stops you.

NEGATIVE SELF-TALK

"Negative self-talk is like a pesky mouse nibbling holes in your motivation and willpower until there's nothing left of either."

W<small>HAT</small> is negative self-talk? It's the subtle conversation you have with yourself in which you tell yourself you're not capable of achieving your goals. It's the little voice in your head that says things like:

- *I can't do this.*
- *It's not going to work.*
- *I won't stick with it. I never do.*
- *There's no way. It's too hard.*
- *I'm too fat.*
- *I hate my thighs.*
- *My butt's too big.*
- *I know I'm going to blow it.*
- *I'll always be fat.*
- *I don't have the willpower.*
- *I'm not ready to change.*

Negative self-talk is not a productive habit. In fact, it's self-defeating, because so often the messages we send ourselves have a way of coming true. Is negative self-talk indicative of an underlying desire to fail? Probably not. More likely, it's an indication of a powerful emotional desire to **not** fail. Negative self-talk is part of a defense mechanism we develop to protect us from having to experience feelings or emotions we believe will be unpleasant. It's an easy way out; a way to talk ourselves out of moving in a direction that may take us where we don't want to go. *"I can't do it"* is really another way of saying *"I don't want to deal with the experience of doing it."*

EMOTION-REACTION THINKING

People who frequently use negative self-talk are strongly influenced by their emotions. Quite often, their decisions are dictated by anticipated feelings. Before truly making a decision, they prefer to "test the waters" a bit to see what it would feel like if they really did commit themselves. In their minds, they pretend they've made their decision. This results in an emotional reaction. Depending on the particular reaction, they choose whether to take action or not. When the feeling is unpleasant, negative self-talk is used to avoid carrying through with the decision.

This form of thinking is called **emotion-reaction thinking**: thoughts produce internal emotions; these emotions generate reactions, and re-actions ultimately determine final action. It's a cycle commonly experienced by people struggling with their weight.

Thought: *I really want to change this body of mine.*

Emotion: *I'm tired of feeling fat. I don't feel good about myself when I'm this overfat.*

Reaction: *Frustration*

Negative   *I'm such a blob. I'm never going*
Self-Talk: *to get rid of this excess fat.*

Action: *No forward movement.*

*

Thought: *I need to go on a diet and get back in to exercising.*

Emotion: *Dieting is so hard for me. I re-member the last time I went on a diet. It was really tough giving up the foods I enjoy. I felt deprived alot of the time.*

Reaction: *Anxiety*

Negative Self-Talk:	*I won't stick with it. I never do. Why bother trying?*
Action:	*No forward movement.*

*

Thought:	*I did have some good luck with that one program I tried last year. Why didn't I keep it up?*
Emotion:	*I was doing so well, and then I just let it all slip away. It was terrible. I knew everyone was watching me.*
Reaction:	*Disappointment, guilt*
Negative Self-Talk:	*I don't have the strength to go through that again.*
Action:	*No forward movement.*

*

Thought:	*Do I really have the energy and motivation to go through all of that again?*
Emotion:	*I remember how lousy I felt when I first started exercising. I've got*

> to go through that stage again.
> Ugh. I'm not sure I could handle
> that right now.

Reaction: *Doubt, anxiety*

Negative   *I can't do it. I guess I'm just*
Self-Talk: *meant to be fat.*

Action: *No forward movement.*

*

In each of these examples, the emotional reaction attached to the thought of weight control was so undesirable, that the decision was ultimately made to not take action. The **negative self-talk is a symptom of emotion-reaction thinking**. It is the end product of a series of thoughts, emotions and reactions.

The major flaw in emotion-reaction thinking is the assumption that because a past experience evoked a certain feeling, repeating that experience will reproduce the same feeling, e.g. because losing fat has been frustrating in the past, it will be frustrating next time.

The truth is, your history doesn't have to repeat itself, IF YOU DON'T WANT IT TO. You have the ability to choose which feelings and emotions you want to own. If you don't like feeling guilty, frustrated, doubtful, or anxious, then make a decision not to. You, and no one else, must consciously decide what you want. Once you know what you want, you can begin the process of making it a reality. Remember, one of the keys to change is true desire.

ON THE LOOKOUT FOR NEGATIVE SELF-TALK

You can break the emotion-reaction cycle by learning to interrupt the cycle before you get to the point of negative self-talk. Unfortunately, it's difficult to do, especially if emotion-reaction thinking is a long-established habit. Emotion-reaction thinking is like a well-worn trail branching off the main path. When you come upon this path your natural tendency is to follow it. Your sense tells you you've been there before. What it doesn't tell you is that this path is a dead-end.

Most of the time you're not even aware you're traveling on the emotion-reaction path. In your mind you zip right on from your initial thought, barely noticing the emotion that follows. You step around your reaction just in time to hear your negative self-talk crashing around you. By the time you realize what's going on, you bump into the wall at the end of the trail. There's no way you can go any further. All forward movement stops.

RETRACING

The best way to get yourself moving forward

again is to mentally retrace your steps and work your way back to the main path. To start, you must keep an open ear at all times for negative self-talk. Fortunately, because negative self-talk is usually charged with plenty of emotional energy, it's presence is hard to miss. It's critical that you not let it slip by. At first, it will take awhile before you recognize negative self-talk. You may not even realize you did it until later in the day. The length of time between when the negative self-talk occurs and when you realize it is not important. More important is what you do once you recognize its presence.

Take a moment to face your negative self-talk head on. What are the exact words you're telling yourself? Do you honestly desire to fail? Do you really believe you can't succeed? Think about it until you feel secure rejecting your negative self-talk.

Next, trace your way back to the reaction that preceded your negative self-talk. What was your reaction? Doubt? Guilt? Anxiety? Frustration? Do you want to "own" these reactions? Do they help or hinder your efforts to change?

Once you've realized how your reactions are impeding your progress, take another step back and try to find the emotions that led to your reaction. What were you feeling before you got to the point of negative self-talk? Try to determine whether your emotional assumptions are reasonable. Are they necessary? Are you arguing for your limitations?

When, in the process of self-reflection, you realize your actions are ruled by your emotions, tell yourself that emotions are not tangible objects. They come and go. Pleasant or unpleasant, they're a part of life.   When you experience an unpleasant feeling or emotion, simply take it for what it is, think about it, try to understand it, learn from it, and move on.   Remember, just because you had an emotional experience the last time you attempted to change doesn't mean you'll experience the same emotion this time. You have the power to either hold onto unpleasant emotions for dear life or send them packing. Once you realize this simple truth, you'll no longer allow fears of unpleasant emotions to prevent you from taking action.

Having gone through this process of retracing, you'll eventually find yourself back to the point of your original thought. At this point, you can start moving forward again on the path to change.

Hopefully, the process of retracing will increase your familiarity with the emotion-reaction path and help you avoid it in the future. If, however, you find yourself stuck on the path again, don't worry about it. Just retrace your way back again. You must go through this process every time you become aware of negative self-talk. It makes no difference how many times you end up retracing. The more experience you get working your way back through emotion-reaction thinking, the more aware you'll become of your thought processes. As you begin to better understand your reasons for negative self-talk, you'll find yourself recognizing it sooner and sooner after it occurs. Eventually, you'll learn to recognize and stop negative self-talk before it's about to happen.

Here's an example of your new, more positive thought process:

*

Negative Self-Talk:	*I can't do it. I guess I'm just meant to be fat.*
Retracing:	*Wait a second. I'm doing it again. What am I feeling right now? What caused the negative self-talk?*
	The last time I tried to lose weight wasn't the greatest experience for me. I guess I'm anxious about getting my hopes up and then failing. I felt so disappointed in myself last time. Guilty is a better word.
	Well, who says the same thing is going to happen again? I must be afraid it will. Right now, though, I want to make a change. I'm tired of feeling this way about myself. I know what I need to do and I believe

I'm capable of doing it. I'm just going to go forward, try my best, and take one day at a time. If blow it, it's no big deal, I'll just keep trying. I'm not going to let my fears control me. I'm in this for the long run. This time it's going to be different!

Action: *Perseverance - Continuing with my Think Light! Plan.*

Remember...

Negative self-talk is a symptom of an unproductive thinking pattern. If you send yourself negative messages you run the risk of making them come true.

You have the ability and freedom to choose whatever feelings and emotions you want to own.

Try not to let fears of unpleasant emotions rule your actions.

The moment you become aware of negative self-talk, you must grab hold of it and take a good hard look at it. Retracing the thoughts and feelings that preceeded your negative self-talk will help you avoid emotion-reaction thinking in the future.

As you begin to better understand your reasons for negative self-talk, you'll find yourself recognizing it sooner and sooner after it occurs. Eventually, you'll learn to recognize and stop negative self-talk before it's about to happen.

Always remember: there's no such thing as cheating. There's only wandering. Wandering is no excuse for quitting or self-punishment. It's not wrong or bad. Wandering is normal.

WANDERING

"Changing your eating and exercise habits is like learning to walk. You're going to fall in the process. You can count on it. When it happens, don't make a big deal out of it. Get up and try again. Failure is a decision not to try anymore."

It's a familiar scenario. The first of the year rolls around and you make a firm commitment to yourself to get back on a program: you'll exercise Monday, Wednesday, and Friday and stick to a 1,000-calorie diet. "This is it," you say. "I'm going to lose those 10 pounds once and for all!" With good intentions you lay down the law, muster up all the self-discipline you can, and proceed according to plan. By your calculations, you should reach your goal weight by the middle of next month. No problem. You can handle it.

Of course, problems do arise. Like the week you can't make it to the gym because your youngest is home with the flu. Or the three-day business trip that includes lunch meetings at fancy French restaurants. What about the ingrown toenail that temporarily makes putting on your exercise shoes an experience worse than torture? What happens to your plan, then? Can you still handle it?

If you're like most people, your reaction when problems or temptations manage to sidetrack you from your structured program is one of disappointment. You feel like all your hard work has been for nought. "I blew it," you say. "And I was doing so well, too. I've ruined everything. Well, it's over now. I didn't make it. There's no going back now. I just don't have the motivation to start back over again." Feeling defeated, you slide off your plan, returning to your old habits. Maybe this spring would be a better time to start...

THE ALL-OR-NOTHING ATTITUDE

This all-or-nothing attitude is the reason why most people have so little success with their weight control programs. It's true that a certain amount of structure and regimentation is helpful. A structured program is appealing since it relieves you of the responsibility of making choices. It also keeps you moving toward your goals. A properly designed structured plan makes good sense. What doesn't make sense, though, is the expectation that you will unwaveringly stick to a structured eating and exercise plan for an extended period of time.

If you begin a weight control program with the assumption that any deviations from your plan will ruin it, you may as well not even begin. No matter how sincere your efforts, things don't always go according to plan. You can count on it. Life is full of unplanned interruptions, distractions, and temptations. The only thing you can predict with certainty is that the unpredictable *will* occur. Your best approach is to prepare for it, keep an open mind, and maintain an attitude of acceptance.

FOLLOWING THE PATH

The Think Light! - Lowfat Living Plan represents the path you must follow to change your eating and exercise habits. Start your journey with an understanding that there will be days ahead where the going will get tough. It's inevitable that events will happen in your life which will take their toll on your motivation and commitment. Just as there will be great days when everything seems to be going your way, there will also be those that leave you wondering why you even got out of bed. Before you begin the journey, tell yourself that no matter what happens along the way, rather than stopping your journey or heading back, you'll **get back on the path as soon as possible and keep moving forward**.

Once you start your journey, expect to be drawn off your path by sights and experiences in the distance. These sights may take any variety of forms - from homemade birthday cakes to lazy vacations in the tropics. Whatever the attraction, keep in mind that it's not wrong or bad to wander off the path. To the contrary, if you suddenly find yourself wandering, enjoy the diversion. Occasional wandering isn't a problem as long as you don't let the diversion keep you from getting back to the path. After you've wandered away from the path, just wander back to it. If you keep moving forward, and don't let obstructions and diversions stop you in your tracks, you'll end up with improved eating and exercise habits.

The advantage of this perspective is that it makes the concept of "cheating" obsolete. People cheat on weight control programs as a way of rebelling against structure and feelings of deprivation. The word "cheating" brings to mind sneaky midnight forays to the refrigerator, or solitary side trips to the ice-cream parlour. Whatever the image, we're conditioned to think of cheating as wrong. It's a bad thing to do. When we catch ourselves cheating, we punish ourselves by feeling guilty, frustrated, or disappointed. Sometimes, we subject ourselves to an even more severe form of punishment; we quit.

Replacing "cheating" with "wandering" takes away the all-or-nothing emphasis on right and wrong. Wandering is a normal phenomenon, whereas cheating implies wrong-doing. If you treat every deviation from your plan as a sign of failure, you won't get too far. When you learn not to pass judgement on yourself for wandering, your journey will be easier and more enjoyable.

Remember...

If you begin a weight control program with the assumption that any deviations from your plan will ruin it, you may as well not begin. The truth is that no matter how hard you try, things don't always go according to plan. It's perfectly normal and acceptable to occasionally deviate from a structured eating and exercise program.

Think of your efforts to change your eating and exercise habits as a journey rather than a task. Expect to have days when you'll be drawn off your path. Occasional wandering isn't a problem as long as you don't let the diversion keep you from getting back to the path.

When you wander off the the path, wander back as soon as you can. The important thing is to keep moving forward and not use wandering as an excuse to give up.

If you want less fat on you, put less fat in you.

LOWFAT LIVING

"Because fat is so prevalent in the foods available to us, the only way to lower our fat intake is to raise our fat consciousness."

FAT IS MORE FATTENING

Which do you think will make you fatter, a hundred calories of table sugar or a hundred calories of safflower oil? Until recently, it was commonly believed that a calorie was a calorie, regardless of where it came from. In other words, a hundred calories of carbohydrate (sugar) is as fattening as a hundred calories of fat (safflower oil).

According to recent research, however, the presumption is wrong. Studies now indicate that calorie for calorie, fat is more fattening than carbohydrate. It appears that the body is more efficient at making body fat from dietary fats (the fat in your diet) than from carbohydrates or proteins. Evidence from both the University of Lausanne in Switzerland and the University of Massachusetts Medical School, indicate that dietary fat converts to body fat much quicker and more easily than does carbohydrate.

Further support for the belief that "fat is more fattening" comes from a study from the University of Vermont where groups of men were intentionally overfed large quantities of food. The men who were overfed a diet high in carbohydrates took seven months to gain 30 pounds. When another group was overfed *fewer* calories from a *high-fat diet*, it took much less time to gain the same amount of weight. The high-fat diet group gained 30 pounds in only three months.

THE FAT CELL THEORY

The explanation for why dietary fat is so fattening has to do with how fat is stored in the body. Under a powerful microscope body fat appears as a mass of tiny spherical sacs. Each sac contains a droplet of oil (fat). These sacs, called *fat cells*, vary in size depending on the amount of fat inside. When we gain body fat, our fat cells fill up with more oil, thereby increasing in size. This process is called *fat storage*. When we lose weight as a result of proper eating and exercise habits, our fat cells decrease in size by releasing their fat stores. This process is referred to as *fat release*.

Eating a diet high in fat appears to encourage fat storage. Following a fatty meal, the levels of fat in the blood increase substantially. When fat cells see lots of fat floating around in the blood, they go crazy, reaching and grabbing for every molecule of fat they can get their chubby little hands on. It's like handing candy to a baby. The cells aren't nearly as greedy for carbohydrates as fats.

Because a high-fat diet increases fat storage, the most effective way to lose body fat is to concentrate on reducing your daily fat intake. Even if you don't consciously reduce your total caloric intake, making the switch to a lowfat diet will usually result in fat loss. In a study conducted at the University of Minnesota, patients maintained their usual caloric intake while reducing fat intake from 39 to 22% over the course of three months. They lost an average of six pounds in the process.

THE 30% SOLUTION

According to large scale dietary surveys, 37 to 42% of the calories consumed by the average American are from fat. With most health professionals suggesting that no more than 30% of your total calories should come from fat, Americans are clearly overdoing it. It's no coincidence that heart disease, cancer, and obesity rank among our nations' most serious health concerns. All three diseases are linked to consumption of a high-fat diet.

Eating less fat is easier said than done. Although people don't usually crave fat like they do sugar, studies do indicate that most people have a strong taste preference for fat. Americans are used to eating fat. We've been raised with it. Fat is responsible for the flavor and texture of our favorite foods; meats, cheeses, eggs, nuts, oils, mayonnaise, sour cream, butter, sauces, creams, gravies, salad dressings, fried foods, pastries, desserts — the list goes on and on.

Most people aren't aware of the amount of fat they eat. Unless you've had your diet analyzed, it's difficult to estimate what your dietary fat percentage is. It's safe to say, though, if you don't consciously think about your fat intake, you're probably eating too much. As an example, let's take a look at a day in the life of a typical person who is not making a conscious effort to reduce fat intake:

Breakfast: (7:00 AM)	Cheese Danish with jelly and a cup of coffee with half-and-half
Snack: (10:00 AM)	Microwave popcorn
Lunch: (12:00 PM)	A typical deli lunch: Ham and Swiss

| | cheese sandwich on whole wheat bread, a small bag of potato chips, a dill pickle and a small (1/2 C) ice cream. |

Dinner
(7:00 PM)

Mixed vegie salad w/ 2 tablespoons of thousand island dressing, a small baked chicken breast, a half cup of steamed broccoli, a half cup of minute rice w/ a Tblsp of margarine, and a cup of Jello for dessert.

Snack
(9:30 PM)

4 graham crackers

How would you rate this menu? Does this sound like an unreasonable amount of food? Would you consider this a high-fat diet? Do you think it's higher than 30%?

Here are the facts:

Total calories	2200
% Fat	48%
% Carbohydrate	38%
% Protein	14%

This is clearly an example of a diet excessively high in fat. Yet, it really didn't seem that unreasonable, did it? The point is, fat calories add up fast, particularly if you're not aware. If you ate like this every day, you'd be in trouble.

The way to make sure your diet is not high in fat is to become a fat-conscious eater. You have to learn to Think Light! before you eat. Your goal is to select foods that are less than 30% fat. In order to do this you must be able to read and understand food labels. Besides listing ingredients, labels give you the information you need to determine how much fat you're about to eat.

A LABEL LESSON

Most of the labels found on foods in your supermarket follow a format established by the Food and Drug Administration (FDA). Here's a quick course in reading nutritional labels:

NUTRITION INFORMATION PER SERVING

Serving Size: This tells you the amount of food that the rest of the label gives information on.

Servings Per Container: This is the number of serving sizes in the entire product container.

Calories: This tells you the total number of calories *in a single serving* of this food.

Protein: This is the weight of protein (in grams) *in a single serving* of this food.

Carbohydrate: This is the weight of carbohydrate (in grams) *in a single serving* of this food.

Fat: This is the weight of fat (in grams) *in a single serving* of this food.

Sodium: This is the weight of the mineral sodium (in milligrams) *in a single serving* of this food.

Potassium: This is the weight of the mineral potassium (in milligrams) *in a single serving* of this food.

PERCENTAGE OF U.S. RECOMMENDED DAILY ALLOWANCES (U.S. RDA) PER SERVING

Vitamins & Minerals are listed in percentages of the U.S. RDA's, rather than actual amounts. The U.S. RDA represents the basic minimum amount of various nutrients needed each day by all people over age four. The U.S. RDA's are rough estimates, so eating slightly less or more than these amounts isn't harmful.

Ingredients are listed in a descending order according to their weight in that food. The first three ingredients listed are typically the highest of all. Keep in mind that fat comes in all different forms. Other names for fat include hydrogenated vegetable shortening, butter, margarine, oil (coconut, safflower, cottonseed, palm, soybean, etc.) lecithin, lard, cream solids, and palm kernel oil. If any of these names appear as one of the first few ingredients on the label, think twice about buying or eating the product.

To determine the fat content of a particular food, you need to look for two important numbers: **Calories per serving,** and the **grams of**

fat per serving. Since you want to know what percentage of the total calories are fat calories, you must first convert the grams of fat into calories. It's easy to do if you can remember that **there are 9 calories in every gram of fat.**

To calculate the fat percentage of the food do the following calculation:

(1) Multiply the number of grams of fat per serving by 9 (9 calories per gram of fat).

(2) Divide this number by the total calories per serving.

(3) The result is the percentage of fat calories.

As an example of how to calculate fat percentage, let's look at a familiar label:

Microwave Popcorn	
Nutrition Information Per Serving	
SERVING SIZE	**1 pouch**
SERVINGS PER CONTAINER	**4**
CALORIES	**200**
PROTEIN (g)	**2**
CARBOHYDRATE (g)	**21**
FAT (g)	**12**

(1)   12 grams fat X 9 calories/gram of fat
       = 108 fat calories

(2)   108 fat calories/200 calories per serving
       = .54 or 54 percent.

(3)   A single serving of microwave popcorn is
       54% fat.

Explanation: There are 12 grams of fat in each serving. Multiply this by 9 since there are 9 calories in every gram of fat and you end up with 108 fat calories. To figure fat percentage, divide 108 by the total calories per serving (200). The result is .54 or 54%. A single serving of this microwave popcorn is 54% fat, 24% higher than the recommended 30% fat limit. This microwave popcorn is too high in fat! Why not try hot-air popped popcorn instead; it's virtually fat-free.

If the fat calories are more than 30% of the total calories, you know this is not a lowfat food. Does that mean you shouldn't eat it? Not necessarily. If there is a lower fat alternative, you should seriously consider it. If not, you can balance this high-fat selection by making sure the other foods you consume during the rest of the day are very low in fat. Remember, your goal is to keep your *total daily fat calories* under 30% of your *total calories*.

UNLABELED EATING

Of course, not everything you eat or drink is going to be labeled. Nutrition labeling is voluntary unless a nutrient is added to a food, or a nutrition claim, such as "low in sodium" or "high in vitamin C," is made for a product. Government surveys indicate that only a little more than half of the processed packaged foods sold today carry nutrition labels.

And what about eating out? By some estimates, the average American eats out 3 1/2 times a week, often spending close to 40% of their food budgets at restaurants. Considering that few restaurants provide information about the nutrition content of their menus, there's no telling how much fat you're eating.

In the absence of nutrition labels, the best you can do to keep your daily fat intake below 30% is learn some basic techniques for cutting down on fat.

LOWFAT LIVING AT HOME

- Use butter or margarine sparingly on your food (e.g. toast).
- Avoid all fried foods.
- Drink low or non-fat milk instead of whole milk.
- Bake, roast, broil, and grill instead of frying or sauteing in oil.

- Use vegetable cooking spray instead of butter or oil when sauteing.
- Use a good set of non-stick cookware.
- Replace regular high-fat cheeses with the lower fat, part-skim variety (e.g. part-skim mozzarella, ricotta, cottage, light cream cheese, etc.).
- Buy the leanest cuts of meat you can find.
- Eat more fish and poultry rather than red meat.
- Remove the skin from poultry before you cook it.
- Trim all visible fat from meat before cooking and eating.
- Apply salad dressing to your salad with a fork.
- Avoid eating nuts as a snack.
- Switch from the premium brands of ice-cream or frozen yogurt to the lower fat varieties.
- Switch to reduced calorie mayonnaise or substitute with low or non-fat yogurt.
- Buy tuna packed in water, not oil. Rinse the tuna under cold running water for roughly 1 minute and drain (rinsing substantially reduces salt content).

LOWERING THE FAT IN RECIPES

- Substitute 2 egg whites for 1 whole egg.
- Use 1/3 to 1/2 the amount of oil called for in most recipes. For texture, replace with apple juice, milk, or yogurt.
- Saute vegetables in dry cooking sherry or wine instead of oil.

- When preparing water for pasta, rice, or vegetables don't add oil or salt.
- Replace lean ground beef with ground turkey.
- Replace sour cream with non-fat yogurt or a blended mixture of low-fat cottage cheese (1 C), lemon juice (1 tsp), and buttermilk (2 Tblsp.)
- Whip plain yogurt with vanilla extract and honey for a desert topping to replace whipped cream.

EATING OUT THE LOWFAT WAY

The most important point to remember when you eat out the lowfat way is: *as a paying customer it's your right to request the way you want your food prepared and served.* Unless you say something in advance, don't count on the cook or your server to look out for your best interests in the fat department. Expect mounds of butter on your pancakes, vegetables, baked potatoes, and bread. Expect ladles of dressing on your salads. Count on cups of creamy sauces on your pasta, fish, or chicken. Restaurants know that most people enjoy the flavor of fat; and they're in the business of giving people what they want. It's really to the restaurant's benefit, as well as yours, to tell them what you want.

What To Say To Your Server

- *I'd like my toast dry.*
- *No butter on the pancakes, please.*
- *Would you please make my omelette with 1 egg and 2 egg whites, instead of 3 eggs?*
- *I'd like my sandwich without mayonnaise, please.*
- *I only want 3 ounces of turkey on my sandwich, thanks.*
- *I'd like the salad dressing on the side, please.*
- *Would you please bring the sauce in a bowl instead of putting it on the fish?*
- *I'd like my baked potato with everything on the side.*
- *Can you steam the vegetables please, no butter?*
- *Can I have my fish broiled without the butter?*
- *Would you please tell the chef to go light on the oil?*
- *May I please have a doggie bag?*

Eating out doesn't mean you have to throw your 30% goal out the window. With a little menu savvy, you can make the right choices at any type of restaurant and still enjoy a healthy, satisfying lowfat meal. On the following pages you'll find some lowfat suggestions and guidelines to take with you the next time you eat out.

MEXICAN FOOD

If you're careful, you can enjoy a satisfying, lowfat meal at a Mexican restaurant. That means avoiding or modifying those menu selections that are heavily laden with oil, lard, or cheese. For example, the tortilla chips placed on the table the moment you sit down are grease traps. A small handful of tortilla chips amounts to 150 calories, over 50% of which are fat calories. Add a couple of ounces of melted cheese, a few olives, and a scoop of guacamole and both the calorie and fat count triples! The solution is to ask your server to remove the tortilla chips from the table. If you want an appetizer, ask for soft corn tortillas instead. They taste especially good if you roll them up and dip them in salsa.

Here are some other lowfat suggestions and reminders for ordering at a Mexican restaurant.

Ceviche (fish marinated in lime juice, vegetables, & spices):

- Good lowfat choice.
- Order with a salad or shredded lettuce.
- Ask for soft corn tortillas and roll your own seafood burritos with ceviche and lettuce.

Tostada (salad served open-faced on fried corn or flour tortilla):

- Order with chicken or fish instead of beef.
- Ask them to not put sour cream on top.
- Request a soft corn tortilla, not a fried one.

- Go light on the guacamole and olives.
- One tostada is usually enough for a satisfying meal.

Taco (folded fried corn tortilla stuffed with variety of goodies):

- Order chicken or fish instead of beef.
- No sour cream, please.
- Ask for soft corn tortillas instead of the fried taco shells.

Burritos (rolled flour tortilla usually stuffed with meat, beans, or cheese and covered with sauce):

- Order chicken, fish, or bean instead of beef or cheese.
- No sour cream, please.
- Ask them not to put extra melted cheese on top.
- Sauce is okay since it's low in fat.

Enchilada (rolled corn tortilla usually stuffed with meat or cheese and baked covered with sauce and shredded cheese)

- Order chicken or fish instead of beef or cheese.
- No sour cream, please.
- Ask them not to melt additional cheese on top of your enchilada.
- Sauce is okay.

Chile Relleno

- High in fat (Egg battered and deep fried.)

Mexican Rice
• High in fat. Ask them not to add oil or lard if possible.

Refried Beans
• Moderately high in fat because they're prepared with lard and served with melted cheese.

CHINESE FOOD

Because many of the selections found on a Chinese restaurant menu are fried in oil, what seems like a reasonable lowfat choice may actually come to the table bathed in fat. Chinese restaurants also tend to go heavy on the salt and sugar. The best you can do to avoid this is be specific when you order. Most Chinese restaurants are amenable to making changes or substitutions. Just remember to tell your server, "No MSG, sugar, oil, or soy sauce, please."

Appetizers
• If you can manage it, skip the appetizers. The usual choices (e.g., egg rolls, won tons, fried noodles, etc.) are extremely high in fat.

Soup
• Pick broth-based soups rather than chowder or cream soups. Ask them not to add oil to your soup, if possible.

Vegetables

- Ask for steamed vegetables, rather than fried. If this is not possible, request that they stir-fry them in chicken broth or water.
- Most of the sauces served with vegetables dishes are relatively low in fat.

Seafood

- Look for baked or broiled items.
- Good selections include baked fillets, braised scallops, Mu Shu shrimp, shrimp in black bean sauce, etc.

Chicken

- Avoid selections that are batter fried (e.g. lemon chicken, sweet and sour, etc.).
- Opt for chicken with vegetables.
- Cashews, peanuts, and almonds all add extra fat to the meal.

Rice & Noodles

- Ask for plain, steamed rice, not fried.
- Ask for boiled noodles, not fried.

Go ahead and splurge with a fortune cookie!

ITALIAN FOOD

Believe it or not, Italian food is probably one of the best choices you can make for lowfat dining.

Pasta, a staple of the Italian diet, is an excellent lowfat food. Serve pasta with the right sauce, a fresh green salad, and a slice of garlic bread and you have a delicious, satisfying lowfat meal that can't be beat!

Appetizers

- Skip the antipasto; it's soaked in oil and full of olives, fatty meats and cheeses.
- A better choice is minestrone soup or a green salad (ask for dressing on the side or try lemon wedges).

Pasta

- Order pasta with marinara sauce (tomato sauce without meat). Ask for it on the side so you can control your portion size.
- Avoid cream or butter sauces.
- If you go for the lasagna, consider sharing your piece with someone else, or eating half and bringing the rest home with you.
- Order ravioli or manicotti stuffed with ricotta cheese and/or spinach rather than meat.
- Substitute a marinara sauce for meat or cream sauce.

Pizza

- Choose thin crusts, instead of the deep dish.
- Reduce the fat content by avoiding olives, extra cheese, sausage, and/or pepperoni.
- Eat your pizza with a fork and knife. It takes longer to eat and you'll fill up on fewer pieces.

Garlic Toast

- Most restaurants soak their garlic toast in butter. Ask your server to toast your bread with garlic and parmesan cheese only. You can add a little butter or margarine if you want to.
- Consider eating breadsticks or Italian bread instead.

SOUP AND SALAD BARS

Some enjoy them because of the type of fare offered. Others find the self-serve, all-you-can-eat approach to their liking. Whatever the reason, soup and salad bars are increasing in popularity, particularly among weight-conscious eaters. Soup and salad bars make it easy to get a healthy, lowfat meal. Unfortunately, they make it just as easy not to. The larger salad bars typically offer a wide selection of "fixins" for your salad, many of which are high in fat. With a little fat-conscious choosing, you can make your trip through the soup and salad gauntlet with your fat quotient intact. Here's how:

Salads

- Start your plate with plenty of lettuce. Lettuce takes up space, leaving less room for the high-fat selections further down the salad bar.
- Cover your lettuce with fresh vegetables.
- Avoid or restrict your selection of tortilla chips,

marinated beans and vegetables, coleslaw,
potato salad, pasta salad, nuts, banana chips,
creamed corn, bacon, croutons, and grated
cheese.

- A single tablespoon of most creamy salad
  dressings is usually about 100 calories, all of
  which are fat. Since most salad bars use 6-8
  oz ladles in their salad dressings it's easy to
  add five or six hundred fat calories to your
  salad.
- Choose lowfat dressings if available or try
  squeezed lemon wedges or rice wine vinegar.

Soups

- Choose broth-based soups rather than cream
  or chowder soups.
- If you choose to have soup and salad, try to
  keep an eye on your portion sizes. A cup of
  soup and a trip through the salad bar is usually
  plenty of food!

Breads/Muffins/Rolls

- They're hard to resist, but most muffins offered
  at soup and salad bars are exceptionally high
  in fat. Treat yourself to one only if your salad
  was built with a watchfull eye for added fat.
- Better choices are whole grain breads or rolls.
- Skip the butter or margarine and learn to
  enjoy the flavor of the bread by itself.

FAST FOOD

Americans part with 50 billion of their hard-earned dollars every year just to eat fast food. That's a lot of burgers and fries. That's also a lot of fat. According to Michael Jacobson, Ph.D., author of *The Fast-Food Guide*, it is especially difficult to find lowfat foods on fast-food menus. The majority of fast foods fall in the 40-50 % fat range, with some going even higher.

Fast Food Facts	Calories	Fat(g)	Fat%
Jack in the Box			
Chicken Supreme	601	36	54
Jumbo Jack	485	26	48
Pasta Seafood Salad	394	22	50
McDonalds			
Filet-O-Fish	435	26	53
McDLT	680	44	58
Ch. McNuggetts	323	20	56
Kentucky Fried			
Extra crispy breast	354	24	60
Carl's Jr.			
Star Burger	530	32	54
Charbroiled Chicken Sandwich	450	14	28
Burger King			
Whopper w/ Cheese	709	45	57

With careful picking and choosing you can, however, eat fast food the lowfat way.

AVOIDING FAST FOOD FAT

- Omit sauces such as mayonnaise, salad dressing, tartar sauce, barbecue sauce, etc.
- Avoid larger sizes (e.g. "deluxe", "super", "double-decker", etc.)
- Stay away from deep fried foods, including fries, chicken, and fish.
- Avoid "extra crispy" coatings.
- Don't eat processed meats such as pepperoni, sausage, and bacon.
- Avoid toppings or cheese sauces offered on baked potatoes.
- Don't eat breakfast at fast-food restaurants. Most fast-food breakfast choices are exceptionally high in fat.
- Order plain hamburgers instead of cheeseburgers.
- Order baked or broiled chicken and fish items.
- Better choices also include baked potatoes, corn-on-the-cob, cheese pizza, and lean roast beef sandwiches.
- Many fast-food restaurants now offer prepared salads or salad bars. If you're heading out for fast-food, select a restaurant with a salad bar.

DELICATESSENS/SANDWICH SHOPS

- Most luncheon meats other than chicken and turkey, are high in fat.

- Ask for no mayonnaise, oil, or sauce.
- Most tuna, shrimp, and egg salads are pre-made with excessive amounts of mayonnaise. Avoid these or ask for small portions.
- Ask for only 3 ounces of meat, preferably chicken or turkey.
- Ask for only an ounce of cheese.
- Watch out for extra mayonnaise in potato salad, carrot salad, pasta salad and coleslaw.
- Skip the chips. Eight ounces of potato chips have 12 to 20 teaspoons of oil in them.
- Choose whole grain breads.
- Stack your sandwich with lettuce, tomatoes, onions, cucumbers, etc.
- Good side dishes include green salad, fruit, lowfat yogurt, rice, soup, baked potato, etc.

COFFEE SHOPS

Breakfast Suggestions:
- Hot or cold cereals with low or non-fat milk.
- English muffins, bagels, whole grain toast (dry or with just a little margarine and jam).
- Fresh fruit plate.
- Lowfat yogurt or cottage cheese with chopped fruit and/or raisins.
- Poached egg on whole grain toast.
- Buckwheat, buttermilk, or sourdough pancakes, or waffles topped with yogurt, fruit, or applesauce (remind the server to leave off the butter or margarine).

AVOIDING THE BREAKFAST FAT

These breakfast foods are typically high in fat:

- Bacon, sausage.
- Granola.
- Pre-buttered toast.
- Hash brown potatoes.
- Fried eggs, Eggs Benedict, Large omelettes.
- French toast.

Remember...

Calorie for calorie, fat is more fattening than carbohydrate or protein.

Every gram of fat is equal to 9 calories.

Of all the calories you consume each day, less than 30% should come from fat.

If a food is more than 30% fat it doesn't mean you shouldn't eat it. Eat a lower fat alternative, whenever possible. Otherwise, balance the high-fat selection by making sure the other foods you eat the rest of the day are much lower than 30% fat.

It is possible to eat out and still keep your fat intake down; however, doing so requires some restaurant savvy on your part.

Eat foods high in carbohydrate and fiber with every meal or snack.

THE CARBO WAY

In case you haven't heard the results of the retrial, the jury came back with a verdict of 'not guilty'. After decades of false imprisonment, the Carbohydrate Family has finally been released from incarceration.

A spokesperson for the Carbohydrate Family had this to say, "No food group has ever been treated as poorly as we have. For years we've stood by, falsely accused, helplessly watching as the world blamed us for crimes we didn't commit. What made it so unbearable was knowing all the while that the truly guilty party remained free. Let this verdict serve notice. Fat Family, we're coming to replace you. And we won't stop until there's less than 30 percent of you left!"

THE DIET OF CHOICE

Fruits, vegetables, grains, cereals, breads, rice, pasta, dried beans, milk and sugars. They're all high in carbohydrates and form the basis for what's considered the diet of choice: the high-carbohydrate/lowfat-diet. No ifs, ands, or buts about it - it's how we're supposed to eat. Over a decade of scientific research is too convincing to think otherwise. The United States Surgeon General, the American Heart Association, and the

National Cancer Institute have said it loud and clear. When we eat a high-carbohydrate-lowfat-diet, our health improves. When we don't, we may develop all sorts of dietary-related diseases, including heart disease, cancer, obesity, or diabetes.

Documented Effects of a High-Carbohydrate/Lowfat Diet:

- **decreases** body fat percentage
- **decreases** the incidence of colon, prostate, or breast cancer
- **decreases** blood cholesterol levels
- **decreases** blood triglyceride levels
- **decreases** blood sugar irregularities
- **increases** regularity
- **increases** feelings of fullness after meals
- **increases** aerobic endurance

Contrary to what you may have heard, carbohydrates don't cause you to gain weight, retain excessive water, or have bad breath. The classic story of the first-year college student who gains weight because of starchy cafeteria carbohydrates just isn't true. In their purest form, rice, potatoes, pasta, bread, and cereal are not fattening foods. However, these same foods become excessively fattening in their "cafeteria-ized" form (e.g. fried rice, baked potatoes with the works, fettucini Alfredo, cheesy garlic bread, granola, etc.)

Regardless of their source, all carbohydrates share one thing in common: through the process of digestion and metabolism, they all get broken down and converted to a simple molecule of sugar called *glucose*. Glucose leaves the digestive tract and enters into the blood where it is made available to all cells of the body. It is the form of fuel most preferred by the body. In fact, the brain and central nervous system depend upon glucose for normal function. If the dietary intake of carbohydrate is cut off, blood glucose levels may initially fall. The lightheadedness and irritability that often accompanies fasting, low carbohydrate diets, or extreme dieting is essentially the brain and central nervous system's response to the drop in blood glucose.

SIMPLE VS. COMPLEX

Carbohydrates are typically classified as **simple** or **complex**. Simple carbohydrates include refined flour, processed cereals, sugars, sweets, and some fruits. In their original form, these foods are already chemically similar to a simple molecule of glucose. Therefore, once consumed they rapidly turn into glucose which quickly enters the blood stream.

Since the body considers glucose such a valuable commodity, the various cells of the body make every effort to get hold of it. When blood glucose levels rise, the body responds by squirting into the blood increased amounts of the hormone *insulin.* Insulin acts as a "glucose doorman", traveling around the body opening cell doors so glucose can get in and go to work. Without insulin to open doors, the glucose molecule is too big and bulky to get into the various cells of the body.

The problem with eating too many simple carbohydrates is that the resulting rapid increase in blood glucose typically leads to an overproduction of insulin. The blood gets so full of busy doormen racing around opening cell doors, that, in a short time, blood glucose levels begin to drop. In other words, the blood glucose "high" is quickly followed by a blood sugar "crash." This drop in blood sugar may explain why people often experience energy lulls and/or sugar cravings shortly after eating a candy bar.

Another drawback of elevated blood glucose and insulin levels is the effect on the body's fat cells. As mentioned earlier, fat cells are the storage depots for body fat. Each cell is a tiny spherical sac filled with oil. When we gain body fat, our fat cells fill up with more oil, thereby increasing in size. When we lose weight through proper diet and exercise, our fat cells decrease in size by releasing their fat stores. When insulin and blood glucose levels are elevated, fat storage **increases** and fat release **decreases**. In the long run, the final result is larger fat cells.

Complex carbohydrates are found in vegetables, dried beans, whole grain cereals, breads, and pastas, and other starchy foods. Because these foods are chemically more complex than simple carbohydrates, they take longer to digest. The digestion and subsequent increase in blood glucose is a much more gradual process. Complex carbohydrates are less likely to produce the erratic changes in insulin and blood glucose levels that occur following consumption of simple carbohydrates.

Most health professionals recommend that the majority of carbohydrates consumed be of the complex, not simple, variety. Unless they were enriched during processing, most simple carbohydrates contain minimal vitamins, minerals, and fiber. For this reason, candies, cakes, pastries, sodas, jellies and cookies are often labeled "empty calories", that is, calories with little or no nutritional value. Complex carbohydrates, on the other hand, are an important source of essential vitamins, minerals, fiber, and protein. Ideally, over half of your daily calories should come from foods high in complex carbohydrates.

FIBER UP

Americans eat an average of 10 to 20 grams of fiber per day.The National Cancer Institute (NCI) recommends that we eat foods which provide 25 to 35 grams of fiber per day. The basis for this recommendation comes from research suggesting a number of beneficial effects of dietary fiber. Recent studies suggest that foods high in fiber may protect against some cancers, particularly cancer of the colon. There is also some evidence that a high-fiber diet lowers blood cholesterol, and thereby reduces the risk of coronary heart disease. In addition, physicians now also recommend a high-fiber diet for their diabetic patients.

In terms of weight control, a high-fiber diet makes good sense. High fiber foods are not only low in calories and fat, they typically are very filling. It would be pretty difficult to eat a thousand calories of broccoli. (It would be even more difficult to get up and walk away from the table afterwards!)

Making the switch to a high-carbohydrate/ lowfat diet will usually increase your daily fiber intake since most complex carbohydrates are high in fiber. However, to meet the NCI recommendations of 25 to 35 grams of fiber per day, you have to make a conscious effort to include high-fiber foods in just about every meal or snack you eat. Below are a number of suggestions for increasing your consumption of foods high in fiber, high in carbohydrates, and low in fat.

BREAKFAST
- Select cold cereals with at least 3 grams of fiber per serving. Recommendations include *Kellogg's* All Bran with Extra Fiber (14 grams), *General Mills* Fiber One (13 grams), *Nabisco* Shredded Wheat with Bran (4 grams), *Kellogg's* Nutri-Grain (3 grams).

- Hot, whole grain cereals are also excellent sources of fiber and complex carbohydrates.
- Choose whole grain breads, bagels, and English muffins. For a delicious treat, top with a thin layer of ricotta cheese and unsweetened applesauce.
- Try buckwheat pancakes & waffles topped with chopped fruit and whipped yogurt.
- Get in the habit of eating the whole fruit instead of just drinking its juice. An apple is more filling and higher in fiber than a 1/2 cup of apple juice, despite having about the same number of calories.

LUNCH

- Choose whole grain rolls and breads for sandwiches (whole wheat, pumpernickel, rye, etc.)
- A bowl of chili, baked beans, or a cup of lentil soup are excellent sources of fiber.
- Eat plenty of fresh fruit and vegetables.

DINNER

- Try using whole grain pasta instead of regular egg noodles.
- Experiment with legumes (dried beans) more often. They're great in soups and casseroles.
- Use wild or brown rice, Kashi, millet, and wheat bulgar instead of white rice.
- Try a vegetable main dish instead of meat at least two or three nights a week.

• Add fiber to ground meat (sauces, burgers, meatloaf, etc) by sprinkling in high-fiber cereals.

SNACKS

- Eat more fruits and vegetables for snacks.
- High-fiber, lowfat crackers that are good for snacking include Ry Krisp, Wasa Crisp Bread, Krisprolls, Ak-maks, Roman Meal Crackers, and whole wheat matzoh.
- Snack on low or non-fat yogurt mixed with chopped fruit and cereal.
- Whole-grain bagels, rolls, and English muffins make excellent snacks.

DESSERTS

- Experiment with whole wheat flour instead of white flour in your dessert recipes.
- Increase fiber by adding oat bran to breads, cookies, cakes, muffins, and pie crusts.
- Sprinkle desserts such as pies, ice-cream, and frozen yogurt with high-fiber cereal for toppings
- Add a tablespoon or two of oat bran to smoothies (mix 1/2 cup juice, 1/2 cup milk, banana, oat bran, and chopped ice in blender).

Remember...

A high-carbohydrate/lowfat diet is a healthy diet.

Foods high in complex carbohydrates such as cereals, breads, rice, pasta, dried beans, and vegetables are not fattening.

The best way to make sure you eat enough fiber is to make a conscious effort to include high-fiber foods with every meal or snack you eat.

Eat less more often.

MEAL FREQUENCY

"Eat regularly, for an empty stomach is not a good political advisor."

Albert Einstein

MOST of us have been raised with the notion that we should eat three "square" meals a day. Our typical pattern is to progressively increase the size of our meals as the day goes on. We usually eat a light breakfast (if we eat one at all), a medium-sized lunch (frequently in restaurants), and a large dinner. If for some reason we miss a meal, our usual pattern is to make up for it by eating more at the next one. We have also been conditioned to believe that snacking between meals is a "no-no". "You'll spoil your supper," our mothers told us.

Unfortunately, we couldn't be more wrong about eating. It seems that our eating patterns are spoiling more than our appetites. Research has determined that several of the most prevalent diseases of our time - obesity, coronary heart disease and diabetes - may be related not only to what and how much we eat, but to when and how often we eat.

Meal frequency, the number of times we eat per day, is believed to have an effect on how much fat we have on our bodies. Researchers have discovered that those individuals who typically eat 4-6 small meals per day have less body fat than those eating 2-3 meals per day, despite the fact the both groups eat roughly the same total number of calories. The more frequent eaters tend to spread their calories out in smaller portions throughout the day.

One particularly interesting study examined 226 children between the ages of 6 and 16, enrolled in three boarding schools. The same daily ration of calories was divided into three, five, or seven portions at the respective schools. In the course of one year, the students in the 3-meal-a-day school were found to have gained more body fat than the students in either of the other two schools.

LARGE MEALS INCREASE FAT STORAGE

While it is not known precisely why eating large, infrequent meals results in increases in body fat, it is likely that the explanation involves changes in blood chemistry that occur in response to eating a large meal. Following a sizable meal, the circulating levels of blood fats and sugars rise considerably. The body responds by going to work "clearing" the blood and delivering these compounds primarily to the liver, muscles, and adipose (fat) tissue to be stored or metabolized.

The increase in blood fat following a large meal presumably encourages fat cells to grab fat from the blood, and therefore grow bigger. It is thought that the individual fat cells may actually adapt to a pattern of large, infrequent meals by becoming more efficient at storing fat.

AVOIDING THE STARVATION SYNDROME

In addition to predisposing us towards weight gain, a meal pattern in which only a few meals are eaten per day may also hamper weight loss. Eating once or twice a day forces the body to face long stretches of time without food.

This type of pattern "tricks" the body into believing it is starving, thereby initiating physiological changes commonly referred to as the "starvation syndrome." The most pronounced change associated with the starvation syndrome is a reduction in the body's resting metabolic rate, or the number of calories the body burns at rest. This phenomenon is a survival mechanism, enabling the body to conserve energy in the face of reduced calorie intake. Since the body is burning fewer calories, the rate of weight loss slows down considerably . The starvation response may explain why it is so difficult to lose weight even when eating very little food.

When you reduce caloric intake to lose fat it

is best to plan the diet so that small meals or snacks are eaten at least 4 to 6 times a day. By eating more frequently, the body's metabolic systems will keep on churning away, making fat loss and weight maintenance easier and less frustrating. Of course, the idea is to choose meals that are light, nutritious, and low in fats and simple sugars.

The number of meals consumed during the day may also have an effect on blood cholesterol and triglyceride levels (two circulating blood fats that have been related to the development of coronary heart disease). Numerous studies have demonstrated that eating three or more lowfat meals per day results in lower cholesterol and triglyceride values than a one or two meal per day pattern.

AVOID EATING LATE AT NIGHT

In addition to eating smaller meals more frequently, try to plan meals so that the largest meal of the day is not eaten late at night. The body's rate of metabolism has a natural cycle of highs and lows, peaking late in the day and dropping to its lowest level during sleep. It makes sense to avoid putting a large meal into your system after 8 or 9:00 at night when your metabolic rate is beginning its downswing. Food eaten earlier in the day has a greater chance of being used for energy rather than being stored as fat.

EAT YOUR BREAKFAST

Perhaps the most important meal of the day is breakfast. A report from U.C.L.A. suggests that breakfast-eaters live longer than breakfast skippers. After studying more than 7,000 people, it was concluded that eating breakfast is one of a number of lifestyle habits linked to longevity. Children who skip breakfast may not perform as well in school as classmates who start the day with a healthy meal. Breakfast eaters may also fare better in controlling their weight. One recent study measured weight loss when people were given all their daily calories in the morning rather than at night. Despite eating the same amount of food, the morning eaters lost more weight than the evening eaters.

People skip breakfasts for a variety of reasons. Among the more common ones are:"I'm not hungry in the morning." "I don't like the food." "If I eat breakfast I get hungry later."

A lack of hunger in the morning may be a result of a large, late-night meal. The solution is to "lighten up" at dinner or wait until midmorning to eat breakfast.

If it's a matter of not liking traditional breakfast foods, there's nothing wrong with eating non-traditional foods. As long as it's a lowfat/high carbohydrate meal it makes no difference what you choose.

If getting hungry shortly after breakfast is the problem, make sure your breakfast isn't high in simple carbohydrates like sugary cereals, rich pastries, or sweetened juices. These rapidly digested foods may be causing the "post-breakfast crash."

MAKING THE SWITCH

If you're used to eating only two or three times per day, making the switch to a more frequent, smaller meal pattern may take some adjustment. It's best to make the change gradually. The most important change to make is to get in the habit of planning your day in advance, packing food so you're certain to have a light nutritious snack available to you in the mid-morning and mid-afternoon hours. Advanced planning is the most effective way to avoid skipping meals or succumbing to high-fat, high-sugar temptations because you're too hungry or rushed to do otherwise. It may take awhile to adjust to this new pattern of eating, but once you do the change will definitely help you toward your lean body goal.

Remember...

People who eat frequent, small meals have less body fat than people who eat large meals in single sittings.

Eating only once or twice a day may hamper fat loss.

Plan your day so dinner is not a large, late-night meal.

Eat your breakfast!

Make aerobic exercise a habit you enjoy.

AEROBIC EXERCISE

"If you want to lose, you have to move. Exercise is the body's best defense against excess body fat."

T IME for a final fact of life. If your goal is to own a lean, healthy body, you must make exercise an enjoyable part of your life – so enjoyable, in fact, that you don't want to miss it. The idea is to make exercise a habit that gives you pleasure, a habit that makes you feel good. Why? Because if exercise feels good and makes you happy, you're going to want to do it, and – more importantly – you're going to stick with it.   Plus, when you combine a positive attitude and healthy eating patterns with a commitment to exercise, you've got all the ingredients for a lean body!

There's no question that exercise and proper eating habits go hand in hand in weight control. Neither one is completely effective for getting rid of excess body fat on its own. The benefits of a consistent exercise routine are easily sabotaged by poor eating habits. Likewise, diet alone is not sufficient to create a lean, toned body.

BODY COMPOSITION

Much of the rationale for combining exercise with proper eating habits comes from studies of the effects of diet and exercise on body composition. The human body is primarily composed of body fat, protein (muscle and organ tissue), bone, and body fluids. For simplicity, researchers categorize body tissues into two types: those that are made of fat, and those that aren't. The latter category, the fat-free tissue, is called *lean body weight* and represents the sum total amount of protein, bone, and body fluids. The total amount of fat tissue is referred to as *body fat weight* .

When a person steps on a scale, their weight reflects the combined total of their lean body weight and their body fat weight. For example, a 125-pound woman could conceivably have 35 pounds of body fat weight and 90 pounds of lean body weight. A smaller woman, with a more muscular body may also weigh 125-pounds. However, only 25 of the 125 pounds are fat, while the remaining 100 pounds are lean body weight.

When most people think about losing weight, what they usually want is to lose excess body fat. The common approach is to go on a diet to shed the pounds. Unfortunately, with dieting alone, the weight that's lost is not just fat. The scale may say you've lost 5 pounds, but it doesn't tell you that 3 1/2 of those lost pounds came from lost protein and water (lean body weight), not fat.

Unless a person is dissatisfied with having too much muscle, there's no reason to try to lose lean body weight. In fact, there's good reason not to. Muscle is responsible for burning a large percentage of the calories a person consumes on a daily basis. Much of the calories burned by muscles comes from fat. If your desire is to get rid of fat, it makes little sense to lose the tissue that's so helpful to the cause.

SAVE THE MUSCLE, BURN THE FAT

The table below shows why combining exercise and proper eating is the most effective way to save muscle and burn fat.

1-Week Body Composition Changes
(estimated for 125 lb., female)

Method	Fat + lost	Lean = lost	Total lost
1000-calorie diet	1/2 lbs	2 1/2 lbs	3 lbs
4 days of exercise	1/2 lbs	0 lbs	1/2 lbs
4 days exercise + 1200-1500 calories per day	1 1/2 lbs	0 lbs	1 1/2 lbs

Cutting back on calories is not the most efficient way to lose excess body fat. When you attempt to lose weight by drastically cutting back on calories, you invite the starvation syndrome. Your body, thinking it's starving, slows down its metabolic rate to conserve energy and minimize weight loss. Much of the weight lost is actually lean body weight, not fat.

Including exercise in a weight control program helps prevent the loss of valuable lean body weight. Physical activity stimulates your muscles, enabling them to maintain or increase their size and strength. Certain types of exercise, when performed for the appropriate length of time, also stimulate fat metabolism. This translates into more fat being burned, not only while exercising, but for some time afterwards while your metabolism remains elevated.

Unfortunately, fat can be pretty stubborn, particularly in certain areas of the body. Getting rid of the stuff takes time. Most studies have found that fat comes off the body at a rate of about 1/2 to 2 pounds per week, depending on the amount of excess fat to lose and the type of exercise and eating patterns adopted. In terms of total weight loss, it is possible to lose at a much quicker pace; however if it's more than 2 pounds per week, you can be sure what you're losing isn't just fat. As a general rule, keeping your weight loss below 2 pounds per week is a good way to make sure you're losing the "right stuff."

AEROBIC EXERCISE: THE "FAT-BURNING" CHOICE

By making exercise a part of your daily routine, you can teach your body to become an efficient "fat-burner" rather than "fat-storer." Not every type of exercise will do the trick, though. The type which burns the most fat is *aerobic exercise.* It uses the body's major muscles in a continuous rhythmic manner for extended periods of time.

Examples of aerobic exercise include aerobic dancing (aerobics), Jazzercise, brisk walking, jogging, cycling, swimming, cross-country skiing, and rowing. If performed on a consistent basis, any of these activities will effectively promote fat loss. Consistency is the key word. Aerobic activities should be performed three to five days per week, for 20 to 60 minutes per session for optimum fat-burning benefit.

If you are not already exercising on a regular basis, it is important to CHECK WITH YOUR PHYSICIAN before starting a fitness program. After a thorough check-up, your physician will most likely recommend that you start slowly, exercising for just twenty minutes, only two or three days per week. As you become more accustomed to physical activity you can gradually increase to longer and more frequent workouts.

THE ADVANTAGES OF RESISTANCE TRAINING

Recent research suggests that the fat-burning effects of aerobic exercise can be enhanced by including a form of exercise in your workouts known as *resistance training.* Examples of resistance training include weight lifting (free weights or machines), isometrics and calisthenics.

Compared to all other types of exercise, resistance training is the most effective method for preserving, as well as increasing, lean body tissue. The combination of aerobic exercise and resistance training helps develop muscles that are particularly effective at metabolizing fat both during and after exercise.

Of course, there are other benefits of resistance training. Resistance training increases muscle strength and tone. This translates into you not only feeling more physically fit, but looking more fit, as well. Stronger muscles also tend to be less prone to injury.

Like any other exercise, you'll get the safest and most effective resistance training workout when you use proper technique and the right equipment. Check with your local health club, wellness facility or exercise equipment store for the names of local certified fitness instructors or personal trainers who can help get you started.

THE CHOICE IS YOURS

Which aerobic exercise is best? Whichever one(s) you enjoy the most. If you select exercise that is boring, painful or unenjoyable for you, you won't stick with it for very long. Try a variety of programs and then choose the one program that's the most fun. The following information will help you decide which program is right for you.

AEROBICS/JAZZERCISE

Pros: Develops aerobic fitness, reduces body fat, tones muscles, and improves flexibility. Exercising with music is fun and enjoyable. Exercising with other people can be motivating. Non-competitive. Can participate all year long since indoors.

Cons: Must travel to participate. Classes available only at scheduled times. Fee per class. May not be appropriate for people with musculoskeletal problems in the lower back, knee, or feet.

Suggestions: Choose classes taught by trained, certified dance-exercise instructors. Wear shoes specifically designed for dance-exercise (aerobics). Reduce the risk of injury by avoiding excessive hopping and jumping on concrete or tile floor.

WALKING/JOGGING

Pros: Develops aerobic fitness and reduces body fat. Can participate anytime (weather permitting). Requires no specific skill or coordination. Great social sport.

Cons: May not be appropriate for people with musculoskeletal problems in the lower back, knee, or feet. Subject to weather limitations (unless on indoor track or treadmill).

Suggestions: Wear shoes specifically designed for jogging or walking. Increase mileage gradually. Wear bright clothing and obey all traffic rules. Consider enjoying the company of a friend or family member.

CYCLING

Pros: Develops aerobic fitness and reduces body fat. Can participate anytime (weather permitting). Low-impact activity. Great social sport.

Cons: Requires purchase of bicycle (regular or stationary). Subject to weather limitations (unless on indoor stationary bicycle). Traffic.

Suggestions: If riding outdoors, wear a bicycle helmet, and bright clothing and obey all traffic rules. Make sure seat height is adjusted properly. Ride with a friend.

SWIMMING

Pros: Develops aerobic fitness, increases muscle tone, and reduces body fat. Can participate anytime (weather permitting). Low-impact activity great for certain musculoskeletal problems.

Cons: Must learn to swim. Requires access to swimming pool. Subject to weather limitations (unless indoor pool is available). Not a social sport.

Suggestions: Wear swimming goggles to protect your eyes. Never swim alone. Talk with a qualified swim instructor for advice on proper swimming technique.

CROSS-COUNTRY SKIING

Pros: Develops aerobic fitness and reduces body fat. Low-impact activity. Great social sport.

Cons: Requires special equipment (cross-country skis, boots and poles or indoor cross-country skiing machine). Subject to weather limitations (unless indoor machine is used).

Suggestions: If outdoors make sure to dress appropriately. Never ski alone.

ROWING

Pros: Develops aerobic fitness, increases muscle tone and reduces body fat. Low-impact activity.

Can participate anytime (assuming you have indoor rowing machine).

Cons: Requires special equipment (boat or rowing machine). Subject to weather limitations and water availability (unless indoor machine is used).   Difficult for most people to row for extended periods of time.

Suggestions: Keep back straight and use the legs for pulling and pushing. Have someone experienced with proper rowing technique give you some pointers.

Here are a few other important considerations to keep in mind when selecting your aerobic exercise program:

Choose an aerobic activity that's consistent with your personality. Are you an outdoor person, or do you prefer being inside? Do you like the idea of working out on an exercise machine? Do you prefer to exercise alone, with another person, or with a group of people? Do you enjoy exercising to music? Thinking about these questions in advance will help you hone in on the aerobic activity that you'll most likely enjoy.

Make exercise convenient. It's no fun having to fight crowds, traffic, and parking just to go get a workout. If exercise is an inconvenience, you're not going to look forward to it. When deciding which program is best for you, consider how easy it is for you to include it in your daily life.

Schedule exercise into your day at a time when you're most likely to do it. Make your workouts a priority in your life by reserving a convenient time for them. If your calendar is marked for a Monday, Wednesday, and Friday aerobics class at 5:15 pm, you'll be sure not to commit to other obligations at that time. And be realistic. Do you really think you'll stick with a program if you have to wake up at 4:00 in the morning every day to do it? You're better off picking a time of day that you can easily devote to exercise.

Always include a proper warm-up and cool-down in your aerobic workouts. Every aerobic workout should begin with a gentle warm-up to gradually and safely prepare your heart and muscles for exercise. A proper warm-up consists of slow, gentle rhythmic movements such as walking, jogging, or dancing in place followed by static (no bouncing) stretching. Ideally, you should move slowly the muscles you're going to move faster later on in the workout. A proper warm-up lasts at least 5 - 10 minutes.

During the final ten minutes of your aerobic

workout remember to gradually taper down your exercise intensity. Rather than coming to an abrupt stop, the goal is to cool down gently and slowly. This allows your heart rate to gradually return towards resting levels and helps your muscles to effectively recover from the workout.

Exercise at the proper intensity. Fat metabolism shuts down at high exercise intensities. To maximize fat loss, aerobic exercise should be performed at a low to moderate intensity. When your aerobic workout becomes so challenging that it's difficult to catch your breath, you're burning carbohydrates, not fat. Besides labored breathing, a burning sensation in your muscles is another indication that you're not burning fat.

HOW TO CORRECTLY MONITOR EXERCISE INTENSITY

The two most common techniques for monitoring exercise intensity are the *target heart rate method* and the *talk test*. The target heart rate method involves periodically checking your heart rate during exercise to make certain you are working at the appropriate intensity, not too hard, yet not too easy. Your desired or target heart rate range is determined by performing the following simple calculations:

(1) Determine your estimated maximum heart rate by subtracting your age from 220.

(2) Multiply this number by .80 and .65 to determine the upper and lower limits of your target heart rate range.

Midway through your aerobic workout, take a moment to check your pulse. To do this, take your index and middle fingers and press lightly at either the neck (carotid artery) or the wrist (radial artery). Count the number of pulses felt for ten seconds. Multiply this number by six to get your exercise heart rate. If you're working at the proper intensity your exercise heart rate should be within your target heart rate range. If your exercise heart rate is too high, slow down. If it's not quite in your desired target heart rate range, go ahead and pick up the pace!

The talk test is quick and easy. If you can comfortably carry on a conversation while exercising, you can safely assume you're not exercising too hard. Ideally, your breathing should be deep and regular. If you feel short of breath or are gasping for air, you're working too hard.

THINK LIGHT AND BE ACTIVE!

Regardless of what your exercise habits are,

living a lean life means being an active person. Keep moving. Make a conscious decision not to sit when you can stand, not to drive when you can walk, not to take the elevator when you can climb the stairs. Make excuses to move, and do it every day of your life. Get in the habit of being active within an hour after you've eaten. Try to take a walk after large meals.

Remember...

The most important point to remember is that your body is designed for activity. The more chances it gets to move, the better it works.

In terms of burning fat, aerobic activities are best. Resistance training adds further benefit.

Find an aerobic activity that's convenient and enjoyable.

Check with your physician before beginning a fitness program.

Always warm-up and cool-down when you work out and be certain you are exercising at the appropriate intensity.

A THINK LIGHT! DAY

"Nothing is really work unless you'd rather be doing something else."

Peter Pan
James Barrie

So far you've heard a lot of recommendations and reminders for living a lowfat life. Hopefully, you've realized that doing so is not a difficult task. The greatest challenge facing you right now is not learning mental visualization. It's not recognizing and stopping negative self-talk. Nor is it accepting the concept of wandering, remembering how to calculate fat percentage, figuring out what to order when you eat out, or planning your day of frequent, small meals. Your greatest challenge isn't even starting an aerobic exercise program.

It may not sound that monumental, but the greatest challenge facing you at this moment is making up your mind whether or not you're going to make the changes necessary to live a lowfat life. You have the tools to make it happen. The question is, are you going to use them? Are you willing to embark upon the path to change; to embrace the unknown, instead of fearing it?

Once you've made this decision, the hard part is over. All that remains before you is doing it.   Granted, there's plenty of work to be done. But, there's no time limit.   And the only person you have to answer to is yourself.

A PREVIEW OF THINK LIGHT! IN ACTION

Maybe you're still not quite certain exactly how to begin. It all sounds reasonable to you, but first you'd like to actually see it in action. How do you apply the THINK LIGHT! principles in real life? What would a typical THINK LIGHT! day really be like?

Probably the best way to illustrate the THINK LIGHT! principles is to follow a day in the life of someone who lives a lowfat life. For example, let's imagine we're watching a woman named Diane...

6:30 AM - The radio alarm switches on, the music volume set just loud enough for Diane to realize it's there.   Diane hears the music, but doesn't make a move to turn it off yet. Instead, she takes a few minutes to THINK LIGHT!.   She pictures herself on her vacation last year in Hawaii. It's early evening and an orange sun is just touching the water on the horizon.   The air feels soft and comfortable against her skin.   She sees herself walking on the beach in her bathing suit, her feet splashing in the warm water. She feels rested, peaceful, and happy. Her body is healthy. She feels her legs, firm and strong from all of the bicycling she's been doing. Her abdomen is flat. She looks at her upper torso moving gracefully and easily. Her arms are lean and well defined. As she lays in bed, Diane visualizes her face. She smiles; not a care in the world...

7:15 AM - Diane has finished showering and dressing for work. Before she heads for the kitchen she remembers that today is Tuesday. She quickly packs her gym bag so she has what she needs for her 5:30 pm aerobics class.

7:20 AM - Diane's Breakfast:

- a bowl of cereal - Product 19 (*Kellogg's*) mixed with Fiber One (*General Mills*)
- lowfat milk
- a whole wheat English muffin with a tablespoon of peanut butter

7:35 AM - Diane packs a brown bag with an apple, 4 Ry Krisp crackers, and a couple of fig bars. She remembers that today is the birthday lunch party for her co-worker. For a moment she thinks about backing out. "Mexican food is so fattening," she thinks to herself. The next moment she decides not to worry about it. "I'll just watch what I order and enjoy the party."

7:50 AM - Diane pulls into the parking lot at work and passes the available parking space in front of the building. She drives to the far side of the lot and parks. She walks to the building and takes the stairs instead of the elevator to her office on the fifth floor.

9:45 AM - Diane reaches into her brown bag and grabs her fig bars for a quick snack.

12:00 PM - Diane joins her co-workers for a birthday lunch celebration at a nearby Mexican food restaurant. She eats a few chips from the basket on the table and decides to order a chicken tostada for lunch. She asks the server to:

- leave off the sour cream and olives.
- serve the tostada on a steamed corn tortilla not a fried one.

Diane asks for water to drink. A short while later the tostada arrives with a big dollop of sour cream on it. Diane scoops the sour cream off with her spoon and puts it on a side dish. She hands the dish to the server.

12:30 PM - After everyone has finished lunch, out comes the birthday cake; a double layered chocolate cake with chocolate icing. Diane asks for a small piece without the ice cream. For a moment she feels a little guilty - but this quickly passes. She makes a mental note that wandering is normal and to go light on dinner tonight. She eats the cake slowly, enjoying the flavor of each bite.

After lunch, Diane asks if anyone wants to walk back to work with her. She gets a taker and the two of them set off at a brisk pace on the four-block walk.

3:45 PM - Diane takes a short break and eats her crackers and her apple.

5:00 PM - Quitting time. Diane heads for her car and drives to the club for the 5:30 aerobics class. The club is just a few miles from work, is reasonably priced, and has some excellent certified instructors.

5:30 PM - Tonight, the 5:30 class is running a little behind schedule, so while she waits, Diane warms up on the stationary cycle. Next to aerobics, bicycling is Diane's favorite form of exercise. During the spring and summer months, Diane likes to ride for an hour after work a couple days a week. She usually takes her aerobics class on Tuesday and Thursday, and gets in a bike ride at least two other days the same week.

Tonight, Diane gets about 25 minutes of aerobic exercise during her aerobics class. During the aerobic segment, Diane periodically checks her pulse to make sure she's working at the right intensity. She knows what her training heart rate is supposed to be. In addition, she works on her muscle strength and endurance during the cal-isthenic portion of class. The class ends with a gentle cool-down period in which everyone gets the chance to stretch out their muscles and improve their flexibility.

6:45 PM - Diane heads home, stopping at the grocery store to pick up a few items for the week. At the store a new product catches her eye - a new type of whole grain crackers. She pulls the box from the shelf and looks at the label to see how much fat is in it. The label tells her there's six grams of fat in each 115 calorie serving (4 crackers). She quickly figures out that six grams of fat is equal to 54 calories and that this product is over 50% fat (she rounds off 115 to 100 and 54 to 50 and then divides 50 by 100). She decides not to buy the new crackers since there are better lowfat alternatives available.

Once home, she starts a pot of water boiling for some pasta (no butter or salt), and heats up some *Ragu* tomato sauce. She tosses some chopped carrots, zucchini, and mushrooms into the sauce. She throws together a small salad and adds a teaspoon of reduced-calorie dressing. Finally, she toasts a slice of french bread with a thin layer of margarine, garlic powder, and Parmesan cheese on top.

7:20 PM - Diane sits down and enjoys her dinner.

8:45 PM - In the mood for a snack, Diane munches on a couple of graham crackers and drinks a small glass of lowfat milk.

THE FINAL ANALYSIS

Diane is on the right track. Here's why:

- She started her day feeling good about herself and her body.
- She planned out her day, making sure she had the clothes she needed for her 5:30 aerobics class.
- She ate a healthy breakfast that included complex carbohydrates and fiber.
- She made sure she had healthy snacks available to her so it was easy to stick with a frequent, small meal eating plan.
- She thought about being active during the day and managed to squeeze in extra movement by parking further away from the building, taking the stairs, and making the short walk back to work from the restaurant.
- She made intelligent lowfat choices at the restaurant.
- She didn't belittle herself for wandering a bit at lunch. She had some chips, but still used good judgement ordering lunch. She enjoyed dessert and acknowledged to herself that she would compensate by eating less fat later on.
- She ate an afternoon snack high in fiber.
- She exercised safely and intelligently.
- She read labels at the store and chose not to purchase an item high in fat.
- She ate a healthy, lowfat, high-carbohydrate dinner and enjoyed a small snack later on.

THINK LIGHT!

Even if your lifestyle is different from Diane's, hopefully the example will help you get a better idea of the THINK LIGHT! patterns and habits that make up lowfat living. It's up to you to make the habits fit into your life. When you do, you'll feel and see the difference. And you'll know you've made the right choice.

Have a pleasant journey!

FOOD TABLE
(Calories - Fat - Fiber)

$\mathbf{T}$HE table on the following pages lists the calories, fat content (in grams), fat percentage, and fiber content (in grams) for over 400 food items. Use this information to evaluate your present eating habits and as a guide for choosing healthy, lowfat/high-fiber foods.

*	indicates that one serving of this item contains less than 1 gram of fat
•	indicates that the fat percentage of this item is negligible
NA	indicates that the fiber content of this item is 'Not Available'
trace	indicates that the fiber content of this item is negligible.

FOOD ITEM	AMT.	CALS.	FAT (g)	FAT (%)	FIBER (g)
Vegetables & Legumes					
Alfalfa sprouts	1/2 C	8	*	•	0.5
Artichoke: boiled	1 med	53	*	•	1.1
Artichoke hearts	1/2 C	32	*	•	0.9
Asparagus	1/2 C	22	*	•	0.8
Avocado: fresh	1/2 med	162	15	83%	2.1
Bamboo shoots	1/2 C	21	*	•	2.0
Beans: green, raw	1/2 C	17	*	•	1.2
Bean sprouts	1/2 C	40	*	•	10.0
Beans: w/ pork, canned	1/2 C	145	3	19%	10.0
Beans, refried	1/2 C	110	1	8%	NA
Beets: sliced	1/2 C	30	*	•	0.7
Broccoli: raw	1/2 C	12	*	•	0.6
Brussel sprouts	1/2 C	30	*	•	1.1
Cabbage: shredded, raw	1/2 C	5	*	•	0.2
Carrots: raw	1/2 C	24	*	•	0.8
Cauliflower: raw, sliced	1/2 C	12	*	•	0.4
Celery: raw	1/2 C	9	*	•	0.5
Coleslaw	1/2 C	59	5	76%	1.7
Corn:					
canned, drained	1/2 C	66	*	•	1.1
on the cob	1 med	83	*	•	4.3
Cucumber: raw	1/2 C	7	*	•	0.3
Eggplant: peeled, diced	1/2 C	11	*	•	0.6
Garbanzo beans	1/2 C	360	5	13%	5.0
Green pepper	1/2 C	12	*	•	0.6
Jicama	1/2 C	20	*	•	0.4
Kidney beans: cooked	1/2 C	109	*	•	1.4
Lentils: cooked	1/2 C	101	*	•	1.1
Lettuce	1/2 C	4	*	•	0.3
Lima beans: canned	1/2 C	104	*	•	3.6
Mushrooms: raw, sliced	1/2 C	9	*	•	0.3
Okra: raw	1/2 C	19	*	•	0.5
Onions: raw, sliced	1/2 C	27	*	•	0.6
Parsley: fresh, chopped	1/2 C	10	*	•	0.4
Peas: blackeyed, cooked	1/2 C	129	*	•	1.5
Peas: green, canned	1/2 C	59	*	•	3.5
Peas: split, cooked	1/2 C	115	*	•	0.4
Pickles: dill	1 large	15	*	•	0.7
Pinto beans: cooked	1/2 C	183	*	•	1.5

FOOD ITEM	AMT.	CALS.	FAT (g)	FAT (%)	FIBER (g)
Potatoes:					
baked with skin	1 med	147	*	•	0.9
boiled, with skin	1/2 C	68	*	•	0.3
chip	1 oz	149	10	60%	0.4
French fried	20	222	8.9	36%	0.7
hasbrowns	1/2 C	170	9	48%	0.4
Pumpkin, canned	1/2 C	41	*	•	2.0
Radishes	1/2 C	10	*	•	0.3
Relish, sweet	2 T	42	*	•	2.4
Sauerkraut, canned	1/2 C	22	*	•	1.3
Soybeans, cooked	1/2 C	38	2	47%	0.9
Spinach: fresh, chopped	1/2 C	6	*	•	0.9
Spinach, cooked	1/2 C	21	*	•	1.7
Sweet potatoes:					
boiled, peeled	1/2 C	103	*	•	1.8
canned, drained	1/2 C	106	*	•	0.5
Squash,butternut, baked	1/2 C	41	*	•	1.3
Squash, spag., cooked	1/2 C	23	*	•	1.1
Tomatoes: raw	1 med	24	*	•	1.0
Tomatoes, canned	1/2 C	24	*	•	0.8
Tomato juice	1 C	43	*	•	1.0
Tomato sauce	1/2 C	37	*	•	0.9
Turnips: boiled	1/2 C	14	*	•	0.6
Water chestnuts, raw	1/2 C	66	*	•	0.5
Watercress: fresh, cut	1/2 C	2	*	•	0.1
Zucchini, cooked	1/2 C	14	*	•	0.5

Fruits & Fruit Juices

FOOD ITEM	AMT.	CALS.	FAT (g)	FAT (%)	FIBER (g)
Apple: fresh, unpeeled	1 med	81	*	•	2.8
Apple juice	1 C	120	*	•	0.6
Applesauce: unsweetened	1/2 C	53	*	•	1.0
Apricots:				•	
canned, heavy syrup	1/2 C	107	*	•	0.5
dried	1/2 C	155	*	•	1.9
fresh, whole	1 med	17	*	•	0.5
Banana	1 med	140	*	•	2.1
Blueberries: unsweetened	1/2 C	41	*	•	2.2
Boysenberries: Unsweetened	1/2 C	33	*	•	1.8
Cantaloupe	1/2 ave	94	*	•	0.9
Cherries	1/2 C	52	*	•	1.1

FOOD ITEM	AMT.	CALS.	FAT (g)	FAT (%)	FIBER (g)
Cranberries, raw	1/2 C	23	*	•	0.6
Cranberry juice cocktail	1 C	144	*	•	trace
Cranberry sauce: canned	1/2 C	202	*	•	0.3
Dates: dried, pitted	1/2 C	245	*	•	4.5
Fig, raw	1	47	*	•	0.8
Figs, dried, raw	1/2 C	254	1.2	4%	4.8
Fruit cocktail: light syrup	1/2 C	72	*	•	1.4
Fruit cocktail: water	1/2 C	40	*	•	0.6
Grape juice	1 C	152	*	•	trace
Grapes: seedless	1/2 C	57	*	•	1.3
Grapefruit: fresh	1 half	37	*	•	0.3
Grapefruit juice	1 C	96	*	•	0.0
Honeydew melon	1/10	46	*	•	0.8
Kiwi	1 med	46	*	•	0.8
Lemon	1 med	17	*	•	0.2
Lemon juice	1 C	60	*	•	trace
Lemonade: frozen	1 C	105	*	•	0.0
Mango	1/2	68	*	•	1.1
Nectarine	1 ave	67	*	•	0.5
Olives:					
black	10	61	6.5	96%	0.8
green	10	45	5	100%	0.6
Orange	1 med	62	*	•	2.6
Orange juice, fresh	1 C	111	*	•	0.2
Orange, mandarin	1/2 C	46	*	•	0.1
Papaya	1/2	59	*	•	1.4
Peaches:					
canned/heavy syrup	1/2 C	95	*	•	0.4
canned/own juice	1/2 C	54	*	•	0.6
fresh	1 med	37	*	•	0.5
Pears:					
canned/heavy syrup	1/2 C	94	*	•	0.8
canned/own juice	1/2 C	62	*	•	1.1
fresh	1 ave	98	*	•	4.1
Pineapple:					
canned/heavy syrup	1/2 C	100	*	•	0.6
canned/own juice	1/2 C	75	*	•	0.9
fresh, diced	1/2 C	39	*	•	1.2
Pineapple juice:unsweet.	1 C	139	*	•	0.3
Plums	1 med	36	*	•	0.4

FOOD ITEM	AMT.	CALS.	FAT (g)	FAT (%)	FIBER (g)
Prunes:					
raw	1/2 C	195	*	•	13.0
stewed, unsweet.	1/2	113	*	•	7.3
Prune juice	1 C	181	*	•	0.0
Raisins	1/2 C	247	*	•	1.1
Raspberries					
fresh	1/2 C	31	*	•	3.0
frozen, sweetened	1/2 C	128	*	•	2.8
Rhubarb: stewed, sweet.	1/2 C	140	*	•	1.0
Strawberries:					
raw	1/2 C	23	*	•	1.4
frozen, sweetened	1/2 C	100	*	•	0.8
Tangerine	1 med	37	*	•	0.3
Watermelon, diced	1/2 C	25	*	•	0.2

Breads & Pasta

FOOD ITEM	AMT.	CALS.	FAT (g)	FAT (%)	FIBER (g)
Bagels, plain or water	1	235	1.1	4%	0.3
Biscuits (baking powder)	1 med	91	2.6	26%	0.2
Bread:					
cornbread, homemade	1 slice	112	5.1	41%	0.2
cracked wheat	1 slice	66	*	•	2.1
french	1 slice	73	*	•	1.3
pita pockets, 6-inch	1	81	*	•	NA
pumpernickel	1 slice	82	*	•	0.3
raisin	1 slice	66	*	•	0.4
rye	1 slice	66	*	•	0.1
sour dough	1 slice	76	*	•	0.6
white	1 slice	68	*	•	0.8
whole wheat	1 slice	56	*	•	2.1
Breadstick, plain	2	24	*	•	NA
Corn muffins	1 med	173	6.1	32%	0.3
Croissants, frozen	1 ave	109	6.1	50%	0.1
Crackers:					
Ak-mak	2 section	58.5	1.2	18%	NA
graham	1 whole	54	1.3	22%	0.2
Krisprolls, Pogens	2	80	1	11%	NA
matzoh	1	119	*	•	NA
melba toast	5 rounds	60	2	30%	NA
rice cakes	1	35	*	•	NA
Ritz	1	18	1	51%	NA

FOOD ITEM	AMT.	CALS.	FAT (g)	FAT (%)	FIBER (g)
Ry-Krisp	1 whole	25	*	•	0.1
saltines	1	13	0.43	30%	0.0
Triscuit	2	42	1.5	32%	NA
Wheat Thins	4	36	1.4	35%	NA
Egg noodles, cooked	1 C	200	2.4	11%	0.2
English muffins, plain	1	135	1.1	7%	0.3
Frankfurter bun	1 med	119	2.2	17%	1.2
Hamburger bun	1 med	119	2.2	17%	1.2
Lasagna noodles, cooked	1.5 oz	158	*	•	0.0
Macaroni/spaghetti, cook	1 C	156	*	•	0.1
Muffin, blueberry	1 ave	147	7	43%	1.3
Muffin, bran	1 large	208	7.8	34%	6.4
Pancake:					
plain or buttermilk	1 med	81	2.7	30%	0.7
Lite, Aunt Jemima	1 med	43	0.7	14%	1.5
Popcorn:					
popped in air	1 C	46	*	•	0.4
popped in oil	1 C	64	3.1	44%	0.5
microwave packaged	1 pouch	200	12	54%	NA
Pretzels:					
sticks	25	145	1.9	12%	NA
twisted, thin	1 oz	109	1.4	12%	0.1
Roll: dinner	1 med	111	2.1	17%	1.1
hard, white	1 med	156	1.6	9%	1.4
whole wheat	1 med	90	1	10%	0.6
Tortilla:					
corn	1 med	67	1.1	15%	0.3
flour	1 med	95	1.8	17%	NA
Waffle, frozen, round	1 med	95	3.2	30%	0.1

Cereals

All Bran, Kellogg's	1 oz	71	*	•	8.5
All Bran w/ Extra Fiber	1 oz	50	1	18%	14.0
Bran Chex, Ralston	1 oz	90	*	•	4.6
40% Bran Flakes, Kellogg's	1 oz	91	*	•	4.0
Cheerios, General Mills	1 oz	111	1.8	15%	1.1
Corn Flakes, Kellogg's	1 oz	109	*	•	0.2
Cream of Wheat	1 C	134	*	•	NA
Fiber One, General Mills	1 oz	60	1	15%	13.0
Granola, Nature Valley	1 oz	126	5	36%	1.1

FOOD ITEM	AMT.	CALS.	FAT (g)	FAT (%)	FIBER (g)
Grape Nuts, Post	1 oz	101	*	•	0.5
Kashi, puffed	1 oz	98	*	•	2.4
100% Natural, Quaker	1 oz	122	5.6	41%	1.0
Nutrigrain, wheat, Kellogg's	1 oz	102	*	•	3.0
Oat Bran Flakes	1 oz	110	2	16%	3.0
Oatmeal, cooked	1 C	145	2.4	15%	2.1
Product 19, Kellogg's	1 oz	107	*	•	0.3
Puffed Rice	1 oz	112	*	•	0.2
Puffed Wheat	1 oz	104	*	•	1.0
Raisin Bran, Kellogg's	1 oz	120	1	8%	5.0
Raisin Bran, Post	1 oz	86	*	•	3.0
Rice Krispies	1 oz	112	*	•	0.0
Shredded Wheat, Nabisco	1 oz	102	*	•	3.0
Shredded Wheat w/Bran,	1 oz	110	1	8%	4.0
Special K, Kellogg's	1 oz	111	*	•	0.2
Total, General Mills	1 oz	98	*	•	2.0
Wheaties	1 oz	98	*	•	2.0

Grains

Barley	1/2 C	392	1.2	3%	1.0
Bulgar, cooked	1/2 C	188	*	•	1.4
Kashi	1/2 C	177	1.2	6%	5.0
Millett	1/2 C	371	3.3	8%	3.6
Rice:					
brown, cooked	1/2 C	73	*	•	0.6
white, cooked	1/2 C	112	*	•	0.1

Dairy Products

Buttermilk	1 C	90	2	20%	0
Cheese:					
American	1 oz	93	7	68%	0
Bleu or Roquefort	1 oz	100	8.2	74%	0
Cheddar	1 oz	114	9	71%	0
Colby	1 oz	112	9	72%	0
Cream	1 oz	99	10	91%	0
Monterey Jack	1 oz	106	8.6	73%	0
Mozzarella, part skim	1 oz	79	4.8	55%	0
Muenster	1 oz	104	8.5	74%	0
Neufchatel	1 oz	74	6.6	80%	0

FOOD ITEM	AMT.	CALS.	FAT (g)	FAT (%)	FIBER (g)
Parmesan	1 oz	129	8.4	59%	0
Provolone	1 oz	100	7.6	68%	0
Ricotta, part skim	1 oz	39	2.2	51%	0
Swiss	1 oz	107	7.8	66%	0
Cottage cheese:					
creamed	1/2 C	117	5.1	39%	0
dry curd	1/2 C	95	*	•	0
1% fat	1/2 C	81	1.2	13%	0
2% fat	1/2 C	102	2.2	19%	0
Cream					
Half and half	1 oz	38	3.3	78%	0
Sour	1 oz	51	5	88%	0
Ice Cream, vanilla					
regular	1 C	455	24	47%	0
rich	1 C	524	36	62%	0
soft-serve	1 C	488	29	53%	0
Ice Milk, vanilla					
regular	1 C	317	9.7	28%	0
soft-serve	1 C	285	6	19%	0
Milk					
evaporated, whole	1 oz	38	2	47%	0
evaporated, skim	1 oz	22	*	•	0
skim/non-fat	1 C	79	*	•	0
1% fat	1 C	104	2.4	21%	0
2% fat	1 C	125	4.4	32%	0
whole, 3%	1 C	138	7.5	49%	0
non-fat, dry	1 oz	100	*	•	0
Pudding, with whole milk	1/2 C	193	6	28%	0.3
Sherbet	1 C	279	1	3%	0
Yogurt					
plain	1 C	137	7.3	48%	0
plain, low-fat	1 C	142	3.5	22%	0
plain, non-fat	1 C	125	*	•	0
fruited, low-fat	1 C	225	2.6		0.3
frozen, all fruit	1/2 C	108	1	8%	NA

Seeds & Nuts

Almonds					
dry-roasted	1 oz	165	15	82%	1.4
raw	1 oz	168	15	80%	1.3

FOOD ITEM	AMT.	CALS.	FAT (g)	FAT (%)	FIBER (g)
Cashew nuts					
oil-roasted	1 oz	161	13	73%	0.4
raw	1 oz	170	15	79%	NA
Coconut, shredded	1 oz	53	4	68%	2.0
Humous	2 T	370	23	56%	NA
Macadamia nuts, roasted	1 oz	200	21	95%	0.5
Mixed nuts, oil-roasted	1 oz	180	17	85%	NA
Peanut butter, smooth	2 T	200	16	72%	2.4
Peanuts, oil-roasted	1 oz	163	14	77%	0.7
Pecans, dry-roasted	1 oz	185	19	92%	0.4
Pistachio nuts, dry roasted	1 oz	162	14	78%	0.5
Pumpkin seeds, whole, roasted	1 oz	152	13	77%	0.6
Sesame seeds, dried	1 oz	163	14	77%	1.3
Soybeans	1 oz	29	1	31%	0.4
Sunflower seeds, shelled	1 oz	162	14	78%	1.2
Tahini	2 T	172	14	73%	1.5
Walnuts, chopped, raw	1 oz	172	16	84%	1.8

Meat, Poultry, Fish, Eggs

FOOD ITEM	AMT.	CALS.	FAT (g)	FAT (%)	FIBER (g)
Bacon, crisp	2 slc	73	6	74%	0
Bacon, Canadian	2 slc	89	4	40%	0
Bass, baked	4 oz	283	19	60%	0
Beef:					
bologna	2 slc	144	13	81%	NA
corned	4 oz	421	34	73%	0
ground	4 oz	324	23	64%	0
rib roast	4 oz	273	15	49%	0
steak	4 oz	235	9	34%	0
Chicken: Fryer baked					
dark meat with skin	4 oz	189	7	33%	0
dark meat only	4 oz	160	4	23%	0
white meat with skin	4 oz	172	5	26%	0
white meat only	4 oz	144	2	13%	0
Chicken: Fryer fried					
dark meat with skin	4 oz	278	16	52%	0
dark meat only	4 oz	249	11	40%	0
white meat with skin	4 oz	266	11	37%	0
white meat only	4 oz	224	7	28%	0
Crab meat:					
canned	4 oz	115	3	23%	NA

FOOD ITEM	AMT.	CALS.	FAT (g)	FAT (%)	FIBER (g)
Crab meat: steamed	4 oz	106	2	17%	NA
Egg: soft or hard cooked	1 lg	119	8	61%	0
Flounder, sole	4 oz	90	1	10%	0
Frankfurter:					
beef	1 ave	183	17	84%	0
turkey	1	102	8	71%	NA
Haddock:					
broiled	4 oz	102	*	•	0
fried	4 oz	187	7	34%	NA
Halibut					
raw	4 oz	114	1	8%	0
broiled w/ butter	4 oz	192	8	38%	0
Ham:					
lean, baked	4 oz	207	12	52%	0
boiled,luncheon meat	4 oz	270	16	53%	0
Lamb:					
chop	4 oz	407	33	73%	0
roast	4 oz	316	24	68%	0
Liver:					
beef	4 oz	260	12	42%	0
calf	4 oz	220	14	57%	0
Lobster: baked or broiled	4 oz	108	2	17%	0
Mackerel: broiled	4 oz	253	19	68%	0
Meatloaf	4 oz	188	10	48%	NA
Oyster, fried & breaded	4 oz	279	17	55%	trace
Pork:					
chop	4 oz	392	31	71%	0
loin	4 oz	287	17	53%	0
sausage	4 oz	454	43	85%	0
Salmon:					
canned	4 oz	160	8	45%	0
raw	4 oz	236	16	61%	0
Scallops:					
fried & breaded	4 oz	222	9	36%	NA
steamed	4 oz	128	1	7%	0
Shrimp:					
canned	4 oz	132	1	7%	0.2
fried	4 oz	255	13	46%	NA
raw	4 oz	110	2	16%	NA
Swordfish:					
broiled with butter	4 oz	185	6	29%	0

FOOD ITEM	AMT.	CALS.	FAT (g)	FAT (%)	FIBER (g)
Swordfish: raw	4 oz	134	4	27%	0
Tuna:					
in oil, drained	4 oz	223	9	36%	0
in water, drained	4 oz	144	*	•	0
Turkey:					
ground	4 oz	260	14	48%	NA
roasted, dark meat,	4 oz	212	8	34%	0
white meat, no skin	4 oz	178	4	20%	0
sausage	4 oz	260	17	59%	NA
Veal cutlet:					
breaded	4 oz	244	9	33%	0
raw	4 oz	186	10	48%	0

Oils, Sauces & Dressings

Barbecue sauce	1 T	12	*	•	0.1
Butter	1 T	102	11	97%	0
Catsup:					
regular	1 T	16	*	•	0.1
lite, Heinz	1 T	8	*	•	0
Cheese spreads	1 T	19	1	47%	NA
Dressings:					
bleu cheese, regular	1 T	77	8	94%	0
bleu cheese, low-cal	1 T	12	*	•	0
French style, regular	1 T	67	6	81%	0
French style, low-cal	1 T	22	*	•	0
Italian style, regular	1 T	69	7	91%	0
Italian style, low-cal	1 T	18	2	100%	0
Russian	1 T	76	8	95%	0
Thous. Island, reg	1 T	59	6	92%	0.3
Thous. Island, low-cal	1 T	24	2	75%	NA
Vinegar & Oil	1 T	72	8	100%	NA
Gravy, brown	1 T	41	4	88%	0
Hollandaise	1 T	44	4	82%	0
Marinara	1 srv	81	*	•	0.5
Margarine:					
regular	1 T	101	11	98%	NA
Fleischmann's Light	1 T	80	8	90%	NA
Mayonnaise:					
regular	1 T	99	11	100%	0
low-calorie	1 T	21	2	86%	0

FOOD ITEM	AMT.	CALS.	FAT (g)	FAT (%)	FIBER (g)
Mustard:					
yellow	1 T	12	*	•	0
brown	1 T	15	*	•	0.2
Oils: all	1 T	120	13	100%	0
Salsa	1 srv	2	*	•	0
Soy	1 T	11	*	•	0
Taco sauce	1 T	6	*	•	NA
Tartar sauce	1 T	74	8	97%	0
Teriyaki	1 srv	19	*	•	0
Vegetable shortening	1 T	113	13	100%	0
Vegetable cooking spray	1/2 oz	28	*	•	NA
Vinegar, cider	1 T	2	*	•	0
White sauce, thick	1 T	33	2	55%	NA

Sugars and Sweets

FOOD ITEM	AMT.	CALS.	FAT (g)	FAT (%)	FIBER (g)
Apple butter	1 T	41	*	•	0.2
Cake:					
angel food, 1/16	1 slc	121	*	•	0
carrot, cc icng	1 slc	178	10	51%	NA
cheese, Sara Lee	1 slc	230	11	43%	0.7
chocolate, no icng	1 slc	143	7	44%	0.1
coffee	1 slc	341	11	29%	0.4
cupcake, plain,no icng	1 ave	91	4	40%	0.1
Candy bars:					
Almond Joy	2 oz	260	14	48%	NA
M & M's	1 pkg	220	10	41%	NA
Snickers	2.2 oz	270	13	43%	NA
Caramels, plain	1 oz	113	3	24%	0
Chocolate:					
milk, plain	1 oz	147	9	55%	0.1
milk, w/ almonds	1 oz	120	8	60%	NA
milk, w/ peanuts	1 oz	159	12	68%	NA
semisweet	1 oz	144	10	63%	0.3
Cookies:					
brownies w/ nuts, 2" sc	1	97	5	46%	0.2
butter	1	23	1	39%	NA
chocolate chip, 2"	1	52	3	52%	0
fig bars, square	1	49	0.78	15%	0.2
gingersnap, 2"	1	29	0.6	18%	0
oatmeal raisin	1	59	2	31%	0.1

FOOD ITEM	AMT.	CALS.	FAT (g)	FAT (%)	FIBER (g)
peanut butter, bar	1	198	10	20%	
sandwhich-type	1	50	2	36%	NA
shortbread	1	37	2	49%	NA
vanilla wafers	1	19	0.6	28%	0
Date Bake fruit bars	1	85	2	21%	2.0
Fi-bar, Nectar	1	110	4	33%	5.0
Fudge, chocolate	1 oz	113	4	32%	0.1
Granola bar, Nectar	1	120	4	30%	3.2
Gumdrops	1 oz	98	*	•	NA
Hard candies	1 oz	109	*	•	0.0
Honey	1 T	64	*	•	trace
Jam or preserves:					
regular	1 T	54	*	•	0.2
low-calorie	1 T	32	*	•	NA
Jelly	1 T	55	*	•	0
Jellybeans	1 oz	104	*	•	NA
Licorice	1 oz	99	*	•	NA
Maple or cane syrup:					
regular	1 T	48	*	•	NA
Lite, Aunt Jemima	1 T	25	*	•	NA
Marshmallows, plain, lg	1	25	*	•	0
Molasses, Blackstrap	1 T	43	*	•	NA
Nutri-Grain bars, Kellogg's	1	120	4	30%	2.0
Pie (with crust):					
Apple, 1/7 of 9"	1 slc	402	19	43%	2.6
Cherry, 1/7	1 slc	462	20	39%	1.8
Coconut cream, frozen	1 slc	270	13	43%	0.2
Custard, 1/7	1 slc	324	18	50%	0.6
Lemon meringue, 1/7	1 slc	399	16	36%	0.6
Pecan, 1/7	1 slc	566	33	52%	0.6
Pumpkin, 1/7	1 slc	287	15	47%	0.7
Strawberry, 1/7	1 slc	282	12	38%	2.7
Sugar: white or brown	1 T	49	*	•	0

Beverages

Beer:					
regular	12 oz	143	*	•	0
light	12 oz	112	*	•	0
Coffee	6 oz	5	*	•	0
Fruit punch	8 oz	107	*	•	NA

FOOD ITEM	AMT.	CALS.	FAT (g)	FAT (%)	FIBER (g)
Gin, rum, vodka, whiskey	1 oz	70	*	•	0
Soft drinks:					
regular	12 oz	145	*	•	0
diet	12 oz	0	*	•	0
Tea	6 oz	2	*	•	0
Wine: table	4 oz	95	*	•	0

LOWFAT LIVING MADE EASY...

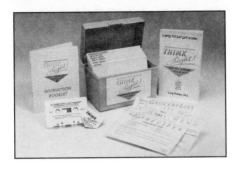

Want some help making the THINK LIGHT! habits part of your life? Try the THINK LIGHT! - Lowfat Living Plan® kit – a unique weight management system that has helped tens of thousands of people successfully adopt a healthier, lowfat approach to eating.

Packaged in an attractive file card box, The THINK LIGHT!® kits include:

- 12 weeks of lowfat, high fiber daily menus
- 12 corresponding weekly grocery lists
- delicious, light recipes
- easy-to-read instruction booklet
- refrigerator magnet
- The THINK LIGHT! audiocassette program

With The THINK LIGHT! - Lowfat Living Plan® you'll lose excess body fat and improve your eating habits at the same time. It's convenient, easy to follow, and full of delicious, wholesome meals, snacks and recipes the whole family will enjoy.

For more information, or to find out where you can get The THINK LIGHT! - Lowfat Living Plan® kit in your area, please call:

1-800-869-6393

(or 1-303-247-3610 outside the US)